Francis Huxley

the dragon

nature of spirit
spirit of nature

With 155 illustrations, 16 in colour

Thames and Hudson

Art and Imagination
General Editor: Jill Purce

Printed in the Netherlands

Contents

The genius of the world

'In times of old,' said a Macedonian story-teller at the turn of this century, 'all things were possible. Why, I remember seeing, as a child, monstrous horned serpents on yonder plain. Where are they now? There also used to be lions and bears, but they have all disappeared before modern guns. The same must have happened to the lamias and the drakoi.'

Those of a sceptical disposition may well nod knowingly at these words, as did the folklorist who recorded them. They may also smile at the drakos himself, a large uncouth monster or giant, very strong and of a childlike disposition, who haunts dragon-springs, as wells are called in his country, and mischievously holds back the waters when women become pregnant. He also attacks bridegrooms on their way to their weddings, though he is easily put to rout by any bride who can claim (as what Greek bride cannot) that she is the lightning's daughter and the thunder's granddaughter, and that she has eaten nine dragons already. Indeed, particulars such as these made the folklorist raise some objections, which the story-teller took to be the usual kind of stupidity that led schoolmasters and learned men to deny the very existence of the dragon – something far more dangerous than bullets, and only to be combatted by the most spirited recounting of its exploits. After one such dazzling performance the folklorist could only enviously remark, 'It was easy to see that he had worked himself into a sincere self-delusion – the privilege of genius and the secret of success.'

A better definition of the dragon – and of the lamia, inasmuch as this sulking glutton is what its consort has come to in these self-righteous days – would be hard to find. For the dragon has haunted the childhood of the human race from time immemorial with its serpent form, its magic jewels and its power to suggest that there is an immortal self in all things. As such it is the animating principle of every place – the *genius loci* of trees and rocks, of pools, rivers, mountains and seas, of bridges and buildings, of men and

Moses leading the Children of Israel through the desert.

5

women and children. Its mode of existence is therefore not something that can be disproved by the usual forms of demonstration, or proved by anything other than the sincere wish that it should be what it suggests it is. What kind of delusion is involved here can only be judged when this wish has come true.

Dragons come in every size and, since they are notoriously promiscuous, in a variety of surprising shapes. The reason for this must be looked for in their parentage, in the elemental mother and father of them all who is responsible for the beginning of things – when all is still in flux and the elements have not yet distinguished themselves. To help us conceive anything of this chaos, many traditions describe the flux as an abyss of water stirred by a fiery spirit whose light allows it to see. In this state, say the Hindu Upanishads, it looks about itself hungrily – the very activity (in Greek, *derkesthai*, to glance dartingly) that gives the dragon its name.

Now it is obvious that when nothing is as yet created, all that a fiery eye can see in the abyss is its own reflection. The sight of this is said to inflame the dragon with the envious desire to engulf it, which it does both by coupling with it sexually and by devouring it whole. For this reason the First Dragon is held to be a One made of two genders – though some say it is made of four androgynous couples – who lust after each other with such incestuous voracity that they can only maintain their separate natures by changing identity. They do this time after time, and through this process of natural selection the myriad forms of life arise from the double One, continuously and without intermission. And, since all these forms descend from the Lord of Progeny, or Prajapati as the Upanishads call him, they all inherit the fate of that lord which is to know life, be known by death, and have progeny on their own account.

This Great Being, which perpetuates itself at the expense of that Other which is its own reflection, is variously described as a man, a horse, a serpent or dragon. All these are said to be dismembered when the world comes into being, and to be reconstituted when the cycle of birth and death comes to its necessary conclusion. This cycle has become famous as the Uroboros or Tail-eater of the alchemists, who saw in it the act of self-fertilization, the container of this new life, and the course of time the cycle takes to return to its beginning. It is the same round celebrated by the Druids when they said that at every spring equinox a concourse of snakes creates an egg out of the interweaving of their eyes. The snakes must have been glass-snakes (also known as blind-worms), since their egg is of glass, and in the shape of a ring. But the original of this ring is none other than the Milky Way, known to the Norse as the Worm of Middle Earth; to the Accadians as the Snake River, or River of the Abyss; to the Greeks as Okeanos the World Stream, and to the Indians as the Path of the Snake and the Bed of the Ganges.

Celtic coins from Bohemia.

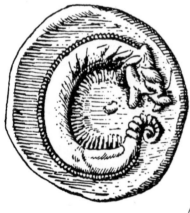

This river of light, basking in the abyss of Heaven, is the genius of our world, and it continues to lay its egg on Earth at the start of every new year. It also does so at the start of every month, inasmuch as the moon is the dragon's most precious wish-fulfilling jewel, reborn however many times it dies. For the dragon is first and foremost a snake, which rejuvenates each time it sloughs its skin, and whose lack of eyelids is responsible for its unsettling gaze. Neither does it have ears, so that the Chinese call it the Deaf One, though they too hold that its vital principle lives in its eyes.

The other dragonish features of snakes consist of their living in holes in the earth, basking in the sun, swimming in water, serpentining over the ground and up trees, having a noxious breath and poisonous sting, being armoured with scales at all points and, folklore has it, possessing as many ribs as there are days in the year. They also swallow their prey whole and vomit up the indigestible bones and horns in which the life of a dead animal is thought to reside, just as the righteous dead will be resurrected at the end of time from the dragon-mouth of Hell. English folklore gives this habit an Uroboric twist in the belief that a snake who eats another snake turns into a dragon, while the nature of this eating can be guessed at in the story of Tiresias, who turned into a woman when he had killed the female of two copulating snakes. He is also said to have been blinded at the sight of Athena bathing naked, which amounts to the same thing; but in compensation he was gifted with second sight and that ancient wisdom the Bible refers to as the knowledge a man has of a woman.

If there is one reason for dragons haunting the imagination, it is surely here: they are the outer aspect of an inner knowledge, both animated by that desire which the Upanishads also call hunger and death. These three aspects of the One form the triple bond of Destiny – a bond the Greeks knew as *telos*, meaning the toils of fate, the issue of a struggle and the completion of things by ritual initiation, by marriage and by death. The bond is also called Time, whose circular nature is found in the archaic belief that the spirits of the dead use the sun, moon and planets as stepping-stones to their place of immortality in the Milky Way (often called the Way of the Dead), whence they redescend to inhabit new bodies upon Earth – the ascent taking place in the sign of Capricorn, the descent in that of Cancer.

The dragon cycle of spirit and flesh is the same that governs the transformation of the four elements into each other. The godfather of this tradition in Europe is Heraclitus, who told how fire turns into water when congealing into earth; which, when liquefied again and heated, evaporates upwards and returns once more to fire. But the doctrine is far-spread; it is summed up in the Chinese *I Ching* or Classic of Change (literally, the Classic of the Chameleon) as the title of the first hexagram. This, usually translated as 'The Creative', is composed of an ideogram showing the sun penetrating the jungle with its rays, which draw up the hidden vapours; the hexagram itself describing the six stages by which the dragon ascends. Here, with the Greeks, the atmospheric cycle is a metaphor for birth, death and rebirth, the spirit being equated with fire and the home of that spirit with the abyss of waters. It is the same in India, where this fire is called Agni and the waters that nourish it, Soma. The Great Sacrifice is accomplished by pouring this water into this fire, so that each turns into the other; and when this is done a Golden Embryo is formed, springing from the root or navel of the Abyss like a lotus flower from its muddy bed.

To understand this evolution we must return to ancient Greece, where every household had its guardian snake and fed it with milk and honeycakes, so that it should bless its devotees with offspring, prosperity and oracular advice. It was in fact the genius of the family tree and, as can be seen on funeral monuments, represented the spirit of dead men – especially of heroes. But here it is no ordinary snake that is figured but one with a beard – a royal beard, to show its virility, its wisdom and its power over all changes of fortune.

The original owner of this beard was Osiris, the first dead man of Egypt to be resurrected, who was also the genius of the kingdom. His myth tells how he was killed by his brother Set, who first lured him into a coffin which he then threw into the Nile. This event was celebrated each year at the rising of the Nile and the sowing of the crops. The coffin floated to Byblos and became a tree, which was fashioned into the central post of the palace there; and from this post Isis, at once the sister and the wife of Osiris, took out the body and brought it back to Egypt where Set emasculated it, and tore it into as many pieces as the moon has phases. The rites celebrated this episode at the time of the spring harvest, when the Nile is at its lowest, and the complete cycle makes Osiris into a figure for the sovereignty of the land, for the Nile and for the agricultural year. Hence the invocation to him as Dragon: 'Thou art great, thou art green in the name of Great Green Waters; lo, thou art round as the Great Circle.'

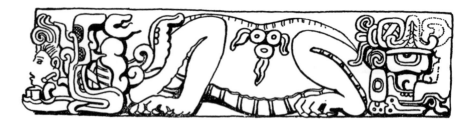

Earth monster. Mayan.

His name in Greece was Uranos; in India, Varuna, who is God of the Foundation, God of Order, of Law and of Death, and Lord of the Causal Waters. Varuna's father is Mud, as befits one who himself is father of the Golden Embryo; his wife is the mother of Liquor, a debased form of Soma. Varuna faces the four directions simultaneously, one of his faces being that of Agni the Fire; and he lives in the City of Starry Night, in a palace that floats in the waters and is surrounded by serpents and rivers. Like Osiris he loses his virility every year, though he takes it back when he has killed his rival to the throne; and as Master of Bonds and Knots (which can kill the disobedient with intestinal and abdominal cramps) he holds everything in a ring.

Varuna in fact means 'the binder', 'the encompasser', 'the concealer', and is associated with words for water, virility, paint and treasure. It is also applied to aquatic animals such as snakes and lizards. Because of this we

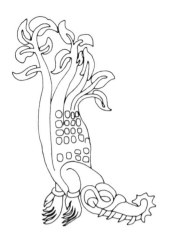

Earth monster. Mayan.

can compare him to the Celestial Iguana of the Maya, or Itzam Na – Itzam meaning iguana and Na, house or woman – whose name also has to do with milk, dew, wax, resin and sap. Itzam Na is bisexual, the male principle being in the sky 'in the midst of the waves' while his consort is the unfaithful Earth, goddess of weaving and painting, whose moon-lover yearly emasculates her spouse. Its two parts are sometimes described as lust and madness on the one hand, darkness and creation on the other; and from their union spring the four iguanas at the corners of the World House – that vast four-poster bed in which the crocodilian Earth-monster floats amongst the water-lilies, the maize growing on her back being nourished by the rain that falls from the canopy above and warmed into life by the solar face of her husband.

> *Mother of the gods, father of the gods, the old god*
> *spread out on the navel of the earth*
> *within the circle of turquoise –*
> *he who dwells in the waters the colour of the bluebird,*
> *he who dwells in the clouds –*
> *the old god, he who inhabits the shadows of the land of the dead,*
> *the lord of fire and time.*

For the iguana is the fire god throughout Central America, its myth telling how it hid the fire in the sky after quarrelling with its wife and mother-in-law, and how the fire was rescued by the opossum – an animal whose pouch makes an excellent nursery for the Embryo growing at the navel of the earth. The Maya, indeed, went so far as to equate the various parts of the hearth with Itzam Na, to bury the placenta of the new-born in its ashes, and to figure Itzam Na as a two-headed monster, the head at the front having the sun in its mouth.

The iguana carries the disparate meanings of fire and water because it enjoys basking in the sun, often in a tree overhanging a river – a tree which the Aztecs saw as one more figure for the Earth-monster – and when disturbed dives into the water below. Nor are the Maya alone in bringing these meanings together. The Chinese say, 'Dragon fire and human fire are opposite. If dragon fire meets wetness it flames, and if it meets water, it burns. If one drives it away with fire it stops burning and its flames are extinguished.' This, in turn, can be paralleled by the alchemical equation of the dragon with the Prime Matter, and with the rule that the washing of a substance is done, not with water, but with fire. The aim of this operation, of course, is to transmute the leaden body of the dragon into gold, within the uterine confines of the hermetic vessel, while its sap is distilled into that fire-water known as Liquor, the daughter of Varuna; as Soma, Amrita, or the elixir of life.

To make all this happen, the dragon-lord of fire and time must not only live in the water but make it. His power, for a start, is usually embodied in a green or blue stone which, when hafted as an axe, was also the sceptre of Mayan kings. This can be used to call up the rain when the Chacs, as the present-day Maya call the four Iguanas of the House, have deserted their pools and rivers during the dry season to sleep overlong in their caves in the

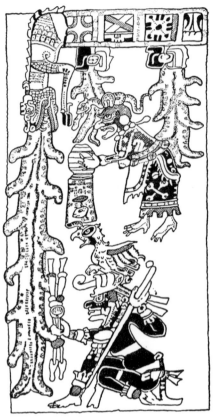

Deer-footed dragon and his consort. Mayan.

hills, causing earthquakes as they toss in their dreams. They then surge out with their water jars, shouting at each other and causing storms whenever a female Chac collides with a cloud. Both sexes are imagined as having the body of a plumed serpent and a human head, which in the male is crowned with antlers. This is because the deer grows its antlers in the rainy season, when the Maya say the sun is being pulled over the sky by a stag, only to have them burnt off when it adulterously puts its head under the skirts of the Earth-monster at the start of the dry season.

The deer is figured as the foreparts of the dragon in the Old World too, no doubt because the shedding of its antlers corresponds to the sloughing of the skin from its serpent tail. But horns are also emblems of virility, so that the goat, the ram, the antelope, the blackbuck and the bull are often substituted for the deer. Likewise the tail of the dragon can as well be that of a lizard, a crocodile, a fish, eel or dolphin as of a snake. This combination of a hot-blooded and a cold-blooded animal aptly sums up the dragon's compound nature of fire and water. It can also be read as a sequence, of dry season followed by wet, or of the three seasons exemplified by the Chimera with its lion body, snake tail, and goat's head perched upon its back.

Though the Chimera does not much look like one, it was certainly a dragon if only because its parents were: its father being Typhon, or Smoking Hurricane, and its mother Echidne the Viper. So was its brother Ladon, who guarded the golden apples of the Hesperides. It also died like one, at the hands of Bellerophon who rode up to it like an early St George on the back of Pegasus: and to clinch matters, Pegasus was the child of another curious kind of dragon, the Gorgon Medusa. However, its most important dragonish feature is its splicing of seasonal changes into one creature, or into one divinity: a feature also found in Proteus the Old Man of the Sea, for instance, his alter ego Nereus, and Thetis the sea-goddess.

These three were famous for their Protean changes, and would give oracles to any who could last them out to the end. Proteus himself was once an Egyptian, since he lived in the Pharos watchtower at the mouth of the Nile; Nereus lived on the river Po, and it was to him that Heracles applied when he was given the task of stealing the golden apples of the Hesperides, since he did not know where they grew. Nereus went through a series of transformations, with Heracles grappling him meanwhile, and at the end told him where to go; and for good measure lent him the brazen Sky Cup for a boat, in which the sun makes its night journey from west to east. As for Thetis, she – when claimed by Peleus as his bride – turned into fire, water, a lion, a serpent, and finally a cuttlefish, which inked him over completely and exhausted her vocabulary. Since he was still holding on to her she was forced to turn back into a woman, and indeed embraced him passionately.

Thetis was one of the Nereids, who are usually figured as being half-human and half-snake. This is an ancient convention, known to the Egyptians and the Babylonians alike, and is seen much later in Christian tradition whenever the Temptation of Eve is painted with a Lucifer whose snake body is topped by a woman's head. The meaning of this can be found in a Syrian text, which first tells of the revolt of Satan when told to serve mankind, and of his fall from heaven (during which, say the alchemists, the green stone of wisdom implanted in his forehead also fell out, becoming the

Emerald Tablet of Hermes Trismegistus; though others say that the Holy Grail was carved from it). The envious Satan then took revenge by tempting Eve in the one form she would not be frightened of – a snake, in which Eve only saw her own likeness. Her fall, the curse put upon childbirth, and the entry of death into the world follow, as in the Bible, complete with her privilege of stepping upon every serpent's head and breaking its teeth.

This is an anti-feminist version of an older tale. We know from the present-day Nasoreans, who take John the Baptist for their patron, that the original Garden had, at its centre, a palm tree entwined by a vine, overlooking a well; and the Nasoreans make no bones about the sexual meaning of these images. The ancient Arabs called this palm tree Tamar, who was also the goddess of childbirth; and the Greeks transplanted it to Delos so that Leto could give birth to Apollo there under its shade, after fleeing from the Python. In these stories it is plain that if a woman sees her own reflection in a snake, this is only because the snake sees itself as the mother of all living, when it is mirrored in a well. This, together with its powers of transformation, are part of its divinity. 'A dragon in the water,' say the Chinese, 'covers himself with five colours (the rainbow), therefore he is a god. If he desires to become small, he assumes the shape of a silkworm, if he desires to become large he lies hidden in the world. If he desires to ascend, he strives towards the clouds; descend, and he enters a deep well. He whose transformations are not limited by days and whose ascending and descending are not limited by time, is called a god.'

The Chinese also had the convention of picturing dragons in Nereid fashion, as can be seen in the mythical emperor Fu Hsi and his consort Nu Kua, who are human to the waist and snake to the tail – their tails intertwining four times to show the constant intermingling of their energies. In their hands they bear, he a compass, she a square and plumb-line, instruments to bring measure into chaos and to found civilization. The convention is used whenever there is a first god to be honoured – even in the case of the pre-Rabelaisian Gargantua, said to have been born as a ten-foot eel with a child's head – or when the sight of water invites one to think of a mermaid with her mirror. Mermaids are of course dangerous creatures, since they drown men in the course of their seductions; and that it is their mirror which is their principal bait comes out with Osiris once more, since he was only lured into his coffin because of his beautiful likeness that had been painted on the lid. Curiously enough the very same fate overtook Quetzalcoatl, the Feathered Serpent of the Aztecs, whose chastity was an affront to his brother Tezcatlipoca or Smoking Mirror. Looking into this mirror Quetzalcoatl was so horrified by his own reflection that he fell into debauchery in order to forget what he had seen, after which his brother presented him with an exactly-fitting coffin.

The moral of these stories comes out in the fact that the 'like' in the word *likeness* originally meant a material appearance and hence, when a man was dead, his corpse. The dead man's spirit, of course, is a dragon, as the Greek genius snake and many stories of dragons haunting grave mounds attest; but we must also remember that the Aztecs, amongst many others, held that 'the hour of parturition is called the hour of death', and that for them the living body was the tomb of the spirit.

For this too the dragon is responsible, as in the many stories of women who conceive when bathing mother-naked in a dragon-haunted stream. This happened to the Celtic princess Ness, who was caught by the Druid Cathbad after she had stripped herself and laid down her weapons on the river's brim. He forced her to marry him, and on the wedding night sent her to the river Conchobar for water, which she strained into her pot through her veil. In the process she netted two small worms, which Cathbad made her swallow; and nine months later she gave birth to the hero Conchobar, who came out of the womb with a worm (another word for a dragon) clutched in each fist.

Cathbad's daughter conceived in the same way, and so did Conchobar's daughter, whose son Cu Chulainn is said to have been fathered by Cathbad himself. These goings on are the sign of some ritual activity connected with a royal line. So it was for the Angevins, whose ancestor Toulouse Hursio encountered a nymph in the woods and got her to marry him on condition that he never enter her room without knocking. He of course did just that on one occasion, so that she flew out of the window and did not return; but she left behind her child, who was the ancestor of Geoffrey of Anjou. He repeated Toulouse Hursio's adventure, but not before his nymph-wife had become the ancestress of the future Henry II of England.

These marriageable nymphs are called *mélusines* in France, a corruption of 'la mère Lucine', the Roman goddess of childbirth. France knows many of them, who are credited with having built numerous castles, all now in ruins; they stay with a man for as long as he observes their taboos, which include

The mélusine.

not touching them with iron (which Chinese dragons notoriously fear also), seeing them naked, or saying the word 'death' in their presence. The taboo broken, they revert to their Nereid shape, all snake below the hips.

Greek peasants speak to this day of the Nereids, daughters of Ocean, as being heartless, teasing, and immensely beautiful. They are always dressed like brides, with a splendid kerchief tied about the head or round their bosoms – a kerchief that is the equivalent of Ness's veil, and of the girdle St Margaret used to halter the dragon defeated by St George. They are also noted for their industry, their singing and their dancing, and though some are known to have married mortals they usually go about their own affairs, which include stealing children, leaving behind their own hideous offspring, and driving out of their wits men who see them bathe. This bath is no more than every Greek bride takes before her wedding, as she did long ago in Troy with a call to the river: 'Scamander, take my virginity!' Any man who then sees her runs the risk of being turned into a stag and torn to pieces by his own hounds, as happened to Actaeon when he saw the naked Artemis. These pieces make up what is now called the constellation of Orion, flanked by Canis Major and Minor, whose setting commemorates the time of year when all men run this risk.

As Actaeon was a king of a sort, and Artemis was amongst other things goddess of childbirth, Nereids are plainly mélusines. To this sisterhood we must add the equally sinister *vouivre*, the wyvern of France, who in addition to a woman's seductive body and serpent tail has the wings of a bat and a large carbuncle between her eyes. This stone she takes out whenever she bathes, and should any passer-by chance upon her thus defenceless he may safely steal the stone, leaving her blind as a glass-worm. One vouivre is reputed for the treasure that she spreads out in the sun, every Palm Sunday; another keeps her treasure in the rocks which open on the same day, and which have been known to close upon an infant whose treasure-seeking mother left it there, for an entire year. Her red carbuncle, indeed, shows that she is a mélusine with a bad temper: the demon rather than the patroness of childbirth.

In France, the parents of this sisterhood are quite proper dragons, who can take on human form when they wish. They live in river caves, near watering-places, where they drown men and eat them; they also catch nursing mothers by floating a golden cup out on the waters, which reminds them so much of themselves that they cannot resist swimming after it. Dragged to the bottom, they are set to nursing baby dragons, and are then set free with a suitable reward. If such a captive takes the eel-paste the dragons give her for food, and rubs it on an eye, she will ever after be able to recognize a dragon who is pretending to be a man. Beware, however, of letting him know this, or he will tear the eye out.

This tale must be extremely ancient, for the Australian aborigines tell of a similar dragon, the Rainbow Snake, who wears a beard upon his chin and lives in a deep pool filled with spirit children. He comes to life whenever two women disturb his repose, one of them nursing an infant and the other menstruating. Their smell is quite enough to arouse him; he lifts his head above the water, swallows the two of them and then rises in a very large storm. When his passion is exhausted you can see him coupled to the Earth

The Mercurial Fountain of the Philosophers.

as that illusory reality, the rainbow, at either end of which the two women are to be seen sitting, much better for their adventure, when it disappears.

Aborigine men can call up the Rainbow Snake once they have become shamans. To be initiated, a man must sit by a pool until its fiery-eyed denizen swallows him whole in one glance, neatly dismembering his body in the process. When he comes to, his initiator puts fragments of rock crystal into his joints which give him the power to cure illness, know the future and make the Rainbow Snake rain. A practised shaman breaks these off from the sky, having sung over the serpent until it erects itself and then mounting it, his disciples in a row behind him, for an exhilarating flight. The only payment required is the life of one of the riders should he fall off, which is customary.

Since dragon stories shoot off in all directions, it is as well to realize that rock crystal is to the aborigines what the Golden Embryo, or Liquor, the daughter of Varuna, is to the Hindus; it is the miraculous token of the fertilizing spirit which overflows as rain if it does not have a cup, or a woman, to contain it. But even women overflow, as is well known to the Toba-Pilaga of South America. They tell of a girl whose menstrual blood did not stop running. 'Will it never come to an end?' they asked. 'Only when my husband is here,' she replied with a laugh – for her husband was a snake coiled in a hole beneath her, who was the father of her many snake-children. When they were killed she, true to form, turned into an iguana.

This is one side of the story. Another side is told by the Bororo, who say that the girl married the man who killed her snake-husband. He gave her a piece of its flesh to cook, but the blood in it went straight through her skin and turned into a little snake in her womb. There it talked her into going into the forest every day so that it could slip out, climb a tree and shake fruit down for its meal, then slipping back into her. The girl complained about this to her brothers who ambushed it on its next sortie, burnt the carcase and scattered the ashes, which grew into plants – into the urucu bush from whose fruit red paint is made, into the resin tree, into maize, cotton and tobacco.

From these stories we can guess that the snake is the kind that sloughs its skin once a month, preferably at the new moon; though if it is an anaconda it does so every nine. The Tukano-Desana are our guides here, for they call the anaconda 'fermentation-placenta' and say that once all mankind was inside it as it drove manfully up a river to its source, the promised land. We would all be there now if the anaconda had not been caught in some great rapids that made it writhe so strongly that we were all shot out of it to all parts of the world.

Anacondas are also notorious for their breath, which stinks of the charnel house. So are poisonous snakes, and crocodiles, the latter being honoured in Egypt as the epitome of the goddess who holds the stars on her leash. But she was to suffer a great reverse at the hands of St George, because she also demanded human sacrifice. At that time she was living in the great swamp near the town of Silene in Libya, whose inhabitants were daily being killed by her pestilential breath. The survivors offered their sons and daughters to appease this dragon, and it so happened that when no child was left but the king's daughter, St George rode by and rescued her. It was the princess who then held the dragon on the leash of her girdle and led it into town, where St

George despatched it; and if his ardour had not all gone into missionary zeal, he would of course have married her and inherited her father's kingdom.

She was luckier than the virgins of Bonny in West Africa, who a hundred years ago were staked out at low water as a monthly offering to the sharks, with no missionary in sight. The same happened in several places in the Pacific, where the girls, chosen for their beauty, were fed to the crocodiles; and in the Punjab, where virgins were nailed to crosses in Plutarch's time, and thrown into the river Hydaspes accompanied by hymns to the Indian Aphrodite. These things have happened everywhere, and whenever they are stopped the story is that someone has killed the dragon. The bait is always a woman, but it is as effective, and more civilized, for the hero to use the illusion of one. Such a hero was Susa No, son of the Creator, who was attracted to Japan by the sound of lamentation coming over the sea. There he found the god of the land weeping over his daughter, the last of eight, who like them was about to be sacrificed to an eight-headed sea-monster. Knowing enough about its appetites, Susa No straightway had a calendrical house built, of eight rooms around a central one, and in each room he placed a vat of saki. He then dressed himself in the girl's clothes and climbed to the roof, where his reflection would fall into the vat in the north-eastern room. The monster came, saw the reflection and swallowed it with the saki. Moving clockwise, Susa No made the other heads follow him and swallow the seven other reflections until the monster was so drunk that he had no difficulty in cutting all its heads off. He was then rewarded in the usual way by taking the princess to wife, becoming king, and in addition having his story – which comes as the oldest poem in the Japanese tongue – remembered until today.

There is no doubt, what is more, that the main lines of this story were really acted out during the festivities at the year's end. When rites are no longer practised, of course, the story lingers on as a kind of dreaded fairy-tale, as has happened at Salzungen in Germany, where a neighbouring lake is known to boil with rage until someone drowns in it. The voice of the water is so insistent that the lake at Madüe can be heard crying, 'Now, come! Now is the time!' while the river Lahne shouts, 'The time is here, the hour is here; where is the man?' and the spring at Eldberg, 'Come down! come down!' And those who hear, obey.

These ancient siren voices can be heard from English rivers also, from the mouths of Nanny Powler, Peg O'Neill and Jenny Greenteeth. The rites in which they figured are lost, but can be guessed at from the story of Fergus mac Roich, who was pleased to go swimming with Queen Medb lying on his breast and her legs about him. He was killed by a blind man at the instigation of her husband Aillil. A more complicated version has Fergus courting Medb's daughter Findabair, and Aillil throwing a golden ring into a pool for Fergus to dive after. The ring is swallowed by a salmon, whose wisdom in those parts is proverbial, and the salmon is caught by Findabair; but there is also a great monster in the pool. As Fergus is naked and unarmed, Findabair dives in after him with his sword, with which he kills the monster. The story ends with Aillil throwing a five-pronged spear at Fergus, who catches it and kills him by return.

Spring is the time for such sexual engagements by the water. So it was too in China, where courtship festivals were celebrated in spring when rivers were in spate, at the place that two met boiling like dragons in heat. (The marriage season was in the autumn.) So it must also have been at Tarascon in France, at the confluence of the Rhône and the Durance, a place once subject to spring floods, and still the home of the monstrous Tarasque. Its festivals are held on Ascension Day, with various guilds making up a boisterous procession during which wine flows, water is liberally splashed about, and the Tarasque – a large carapace with moveable head and tail, carried by three men – amuses the spectators with its antics as it whirls about and plunges amongst them, often causing grievous injuries that are much appreciated by the majority.

The Tarasque is of ancient vintage, having been there when Heracles defeated Tauriscus, king of Gaul: a Celtic monument shows it eating an arm while resting each foreleg on a human head, and sporting a large erection. Heracles must have known how to deal with it, since he had already defeated the river god Achelöus whom Homer called the origin of everything. This was in a contest for the hand of Deianira, daughter of Dionysus, at which Achelöus appeared as a snake with the head of a one-horned bull. This horn Heracles tore off and presented to his father-in-law as a drinking cup, though some say that Amaltheia took it as a replacement for her Horn of Plenty.

Just how he dealt with the Tarasque, however, is not known, though it is likely that he defeated it in St George style. This is the substance of its other feast, at Pentecost, a much tamer affair that has been taken over by the Church: it celebrates the time when St Margaret subdued the Tarasque in its swamp and led it back to town on her girdle, where it was hacked to pieces. The St George story has also spread to many parts of West Africa. The Dagomba, for instance, talk of a drought during which the only water-hole was guarded by a water-buffalo. The hero duly arrives and kills it; he cuts off its horns, the right one of gold and the left of silver, along with its tail, and marries the king's daughter even though she has no legs – doubtless because she was a mélusine to begin with. Among the Koba this buffalo becomes a horse-antelope with a tail of gold, who demands the Great Sacrifice of a princess; the Fulbe say that it is a three-headed monster, and others that it is a curious fish only seen when the rivers are high. South of the Niger the various St Georges disappear and the water-monster lives to take its full significance as the material form of the High God, Amma. In one form Amma is a joined pair of bisexual beings, half-human and half-serpent, with red staring eyes, green skin and jointless, flexible arms. Another form is that of a ram with two sets of genitals. One set is in the usual place, which pisses out the fertilizing rain; the other rises from its head and with this it couples with the sun during its journey through the sky.

The Dogon hold the sun to be a radiant womb made of an eight-fold copper spiral, which sucks up the waters that the ram has let fall. In celebration of this they have the custom of tying a reddened calabash on the heads of rams, which they then let prowl in the marshes. The sight of this great symbol is enough to make the unwary run after it: but the ram shakes the bauble from its head into the water, the pursuer dives in and drowns as the water-spirits suck the blood from his nostrils. For the ram is the hot-blooded incarnation of the water-spirits, and it can be seen plunging in the marshes during every storm, amongst the water-lilies, crying, 'Water is mine!'

When the storm is over, it leaps into the clouds along the rainbow. In addition it has the moon on its forehead, just below the solar crown, in much the same way that the Dagomba buffalo has the sun and moon upon its horns. Its body is the earth, its eyes the stars; its fleece is water and green plants, its hind legs are the larger animals and its forelegs the smaller ones, its tail is the reptiles. It lives, as dragons do, by drawing up and then returning what it has drawn as the breath of the world: and its favourite number is eight.

Eight is one of the Great Numbers, from the days when Noah's Ark took aboard its crew of four human couples, when the Egyptians summed up the first gods into the Ogdoad, the Greeks settled on the octave in music, the Norse had Odin ride upon an eight-legged horse, the Buddha preached the Eight-fold Way that was already being travelled on in the time of the Upanishads, and the Chinese recognized that the Yin and the Yang made one dragon which had the Eight Trigrams for heads. And throughout the Old World, eight was the number of spokes in the solar wheel which, in Europe as in Africa, was set in motion by the ram-headed serpent.

The dual nature of the ram-snake – which makes it the proper ancestor of the binary code and of the number eight – is often represented on Celtic monuments by doubling the ram-snake itself, and showing it in attendance upon a human figure with antlers on its head. In Roman times the inner meaning of these two was shown by substituting for them Apollo, leader of the Muses and destroyer of illness, and Mercury, conductor of souls, diagnoser of hidden ills, and thief. The hidden link between these two is to be found in the antlered figure, Cernunnos by name, who sits between them with a sack of Plutonic gold at his feet, and in the snake belt ending in two rams' heads about his waist. On the north-west coast of America such a belt is the insignia of a warrior, and is thought to deal out thunder and lightning at one moment and a rainbow-like covenant at another. It must also have bridged the two realms of life and death by virtue of its self-reflection, as happened to the Irish hero Conall Cernach, grandson of Conchobar, when he went to rescue his wives, sons and cattle that had been imprisoned in an otherworldly fort. The fort was guarded by a serpent that would let no one enter; but Conall was wearing his belt, into which the serpent darted the moment it saw it, leaving him to take away his own and much treasure besides.

Cernunnos seems to have been the title for such heroes as Conall, and it is of some interest that he wears antlers, like the Mexican Chacs, rather than rams' horns. There are several clues to the meaning of this. For a start, rams' horns are permanent fixtures, unlike antlers, which the French call 'the wood of the stag'. Further, medieval bestiaries tell us that the stag is the enemy of the serpent, and kills it by vomiting water down its hole – no doubt to stop it climbing up the trees on its head as it once had done in Eden. This is indeed more than likely, since in many traditions the stag is the Adam of the land, who disputes for Eve's favours with the serpent. Eve has always found this

rivalry exciting and, as marriage is not her invention, she encourages the pair to cuckold each other – which means, in the old phrase, that she gives them horns.

Cernunnos wears these horns proudly enough since they are the emblems of royalty, even though he knows that they will fall off in the spring, and he die. He then turns into Herne the Hunter, Master of the Woods and Animals, and can be heard when the winter storms come like a pack of dogs in full cry chasing after the souls of the dead. In Scotland this function is taken over by the water-horse or nixie, which has a black coat, a white star on its forehead, a narrow slippery snout ending in a sharp bill, a flowing mane and tail. It is known to seduce and devour young women, appearing to them as a handsome enough young countryman who asks to have his head loused. He lays it on the girl's lap (just as many a St George has

Drawing by T. Johannot for de Musset's 'Le Voyage où il vous plaira'.

done, while waiting for the dragon) and she may recognize who he is by the sand and weed she finds in his hair. The nixie may also come onto a man's land and let itself be tamed by having a cow's halter tied round its neck – this is St Margaret's trick – but once it is loosed, away it goes to the water, stampeding the other horses and drowning them. And it comes to children, offering them its back to ride on: a back that lengthens to take however many children there are. Once they are up there is no coming down for them, except in the other world.

The same water-horses once roamed throughout France, where they were called *dracs*, and when not carrying off their victims they were being ridden by the mélusines, or else leaping at the dawn with such vigour that they left the prints of their hooves in the rock. They should also strike a spring into existence, as Pegasus ('of the wells') did on Mount Helicon when

The Midgard Serpent. Danish.

he took to the air. The drac thus exemplifies the Japanese aphorism: 'In heaven a horse is made into a dragon, among men a dragon is made into a horse.' For the Japanese sacrifice horses at the spring festival, and also when the gods withhold the rain. They are sent to heaven, that is, so that they will become dragons and preside over the change of water into fire and fire back again into water: for the horse only has power over water because it is a solar animal.

The Scots also speak of the water-bull, which they say is harmless. This is a far cry from the days when it carried off Europa through the waves, and before that when its horn, the origin of all things, was torn off its head by Heracles – or from the time when it was Taurus, the Bull of Heaven, overthrown by the Babylonian hero Enkidu, with the help of Gilgamesh. What Enkidu wanted – he can be seen facing Taurus, as the constellation of Orion – was not the Bull's horn but the Tablet of Destiny, otherwise Aldebaran, which is the eye of Taurus. For it was on this tablet that the planet Mercury wrote down the decisions taken by the gods at their spring banquet, and the one who wore it on his breast was king.

It is as well to have this scenario in mind when we come to the first great dragon story, the Babylonian creation epic. It starts with Apsu the Abyss, Mummu his Emanation or Vizier, and Tiamat the Salt Sea, Mother of all. Intermingling their waters they created the gods, couple by couple. Of these, Anu – whose Way is a band around the celestial equator – was chief, and after him his son Ea, called the Likeness or Reflection of Anu. He also bears the Varunian title, Lord of the World Order, and his Way is the southern part of the sky; he is depicted with the foreparts of an antelope and the tail of a fish – our Capricorn.

It was not long before these gods made a commotion in the inner parts of Tiamat, and disturbed the repose of Apsu who, with Mummu's help, plotted their destruction. But Ea, who understands everything, foresaw the danger, poured sleep on Apsu and safely took off Mummu's splendour. This emblem of kingship he put on himself, and founded his Chamber in Apsu's now vacant place, presumably above the prison in which he confined Mummu.

There Ea consorted with Damkina, who became the Danäe of the Greeks and begot the four-eyed Marduk 'from whose lips fire blazed forth', who is the spirit of the planet Jupiter and the embodiment of the storm. Meanwhile Anu's four winds continued to disturb Tiamat, and her other children urged revenge. From these she chose Kingu to be her general, and fashioned eleven monsters – the viper, the dragon, the shark, the great lion, the mad dog, the scorpion man, the storm demon and four nameless others, who with Kingu were the guardians of the twelve months. Then the gods became afraid, until Marduk offered to defeat their enemies on condition that he be king. The gods drank to this plan, and when sober again invested Marduk with power: with the bow-star that is Sirius, the club with which Orion now threatens Taurus, a net that can be seen as the Hyades in the constellation of Taurus, with lightning and four families of winds.

So armed, he drove his chariot to view the insides of Tiamat, and with his gaze put Kingu to confusion. Then, forcing Tiamat's jaws apart with his winds, he shot an arrow into her heart, split her skull, cut her arteries, and divided the abortion of her body, as the text has it, into the upper and lower firmaments. Kingu he imprisoned, taking the Tablet of Destiny from him, and he enthroned himself in the Great Square of Pegasus opposite Apsu. The gods he stationed as stars, so defining the months of the year; and the gods and their enemies having agreed that they could live in peace if only they both had servants to work for them, Marduk cut off Kingu's head and from his blood made mankind. That done, a palace was built for him at Babylon, where he was formally enthroned.

Marduk's exploit is engraved on Babylonian seals, which show a thunder-king standing on a horned dragon with two forelegs and a serpent body. The dragon is not given a name there, and may or may not represent either Tiamat, or Kingu. She certainly had a dragon brood, however, perhaps including other numerous monsters known to the Babylonians – hot wind demons, sickness demons, unicorn dragons and the like, all of them uncertain in their temper.

As for what the exploit is all about, there are several possible kinds of explanation. We know for a start that the creation epic was recited at the New Year festival, at the spring equinox. At this time the length of Hydra would stretch through the night sky, and set at the moment when the sun rose in Aries, heralding the end of the rains. The king, who was Marduk's representative, mounted the seven-levelled ziggurat of Marduk and on its top would celebrate his marriage to the queen, thus inaugurating the calendar of the new year. As the foundations of all civilization are known to have been sanctified with human blood, it is more than likely that Kingu as well as Marduk was acted by a man, and was quite literally beheaded. Moreover, since Babylonia was originally the kingdom of the Sumerians, we may suspect that Kingu was chosen from amongst the members of this then conquered race. They doubtless had had their own spring festival, to celebrate the death and rebirth of the Year Daimon, or Genius, also in literal terms. Since, ritually speaking, a people continue to own the land even when they have been conquered, it was essential for the Babylonians to get the Sumerians' collaboration in invoking the gods of the lands, and perhaps this was done by giving one of them the honour of dying as Kingu, first owner of the Tablet of Destiny.

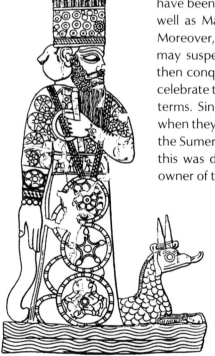

Marduk and the dragon.
Babylonian.

The dragon and its lord. Mayan.

Such are the likely politics of this dragon myth. But there are deeper matters concerned also, for the creation of man from the blood of a victim is recounted, somewhat differently, as part of an incantation to help women in childbirth. It is therefore proper to think of the creation epic as one of conception, pregnancy and birth, with the Tablet of Destiny in some way corresponding to the Golden Embryo of India. Some confirmation here is to be found in Ea, the 'Antelope of the Deep' or 'Goat-fish' whom the Indians call Agni-in-the-Waters and also *makara*, a crocodile-monster with a mammalian head and a lotus stalk issuing from its mouth. Ea as makara is therefore the root of the Golden Embryo itself.

This association of dragons with vegetation is to be found in another Babylonian monster, Humbaba. He was Lord of the Cedar Forest, and roared like the storm-flood with fire in his mouth and death on his breath. Gilgamesh and his comrade Enkidu put an end to him by cutting down his largest tree, in which he must have lived. The curious thing about him, however, is that he was also called Fortress of the Intestines – a title that could easily be given to Varuna – and had a face made out of them. In addition, Humbaba is identified by some as the Water Dog, or the star Procyon of Canis Minor. Some sense can be made of all this from Central and South American myths which speak of an aboriginal Water-Tree bearing the seeds of all life on its branches, and which when cut down loosed the Flood upon the earth. This suggests that the Water-Tree growing in the Fortress of the Intestines has the form of an umbilical cord with a Golden Embryo at one end and the lotus leaf of a placenta at the other.

The Cuna Indians also say of the Water-Tree that it grew above 'God's very own whirlpool'. In the Old World, this was the name given to the constellation of the river Eridanus, which bears away the life from Orion's wounded heel just on the other side of the Milky Way from Procyon. However this may be, a tree above a pool is the regular haunt of dragons, especially when the pool divides into four rivers defining the limits of the earthly paradise. Dante placed this garden on the top of a high mountain, which is also dragon country; others have looked for it in the Ethiopian highlands, the Mountains of the Moon, the Caucasus where Prometheus was chained, or the fabled Mount Meru of India with its naga lords. But the mountain is so high that the final place to look for the garden is in the heavens. The Babylonians saw it there as the Great Square of Pegasus, with a greatly enlarged constellation of Pisces surrounding it on a confluence of four rivers: the abode of Marduk.

Before Marduk got there, however, it had another owner whose nature we can guess at from the fact that the Great Square comprises three stars of Pegasus, whose mother was the Gorgon Medusa, and one of Andromeda, whose would-be ravisher Cetus or the Leviathan is shown on star maps with the two Fish curiously tied to its tail. Now Leviathan is the Hebrew

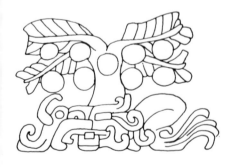

Olmec dragon.

transliteration of a word meaning 'the embracer', 'the confiner', known to the Greeks as Ladon son of Ceto, and brother of Echidne, the Gorgons and the Hesperides; and which came to mean 'lady' as in Leda of the swan and Leto the birth goddess of Delos. The Great Square must then have been the Garden of Tiamat.

Ladon is the name of several rivers, the canonical place for a dragon to see itself in a woman; and, what is more, it is associated with a garden. This is the Garden of the Hesperides, part of the Atlantean kingdom of Atlas, encircled by a great wall and having at its centre a tree bearing the golden fruit which Ladon guarded. Its location has been thought to be at the mouth of the river Ladon on the Gulf of Syrtes in northern Africa. But this is unlikely, for Hesperus marks the western ocean where the Gorgons live and the sun sinks into its watery grave; moreover, the only way that Heracles could find it when given the task of stealing three of the golden fruit was by forcing Nereus to show him the way, and borrowing the sun's Cup to journey in.

Heracles arrived at the garden at a time when Atlas was being punished as a rebel against Zeus, by supporting the weight of heaven on his shoulders. There he shot Ladon with an arrow over the wall, took over Atlas's burden so that Atlas could steal the apples himself, and then tricked him into resuming it. As for Ladon, he was translated to the skies as the Snake of Ophiuchus.

Dragon in its labyrinth. Italian.

We can now locate four of the main dragon stations in the sky: the water-monster Hydra is in one hemisphere, its head close to the Water-Dog of Procyon, and the Garden is the Great Square in the other; the contenders for the apples standing at opposite limbs of the Milky Way, as if over the wall from each other, one at Orion – the dragon as man – and the other at Ophiuchus, the man as dragon. What is confusing is that the dragon of one story has slipped into the scenario of another, apparently different one, while his owner points the way to a third story. But there is no doubt that all these stories are about the same thing. We know, for a start, that Ophiuchus is also Asclepius, and that *he* was put into the stars after Zeus had killed him for trying to bring Orion back to life; we also know that the medicine he used was a drop of Gorgon's blood, collected when her arteries had been severed by the decapitating sword of Perseus. The same stroke freed Pegasus, who had been begotten on the Gorgon by Poseidon; and as it is Pegasus who gives his name to the Great Square of the heavenly garden, it is obviously time to tell the story of how all this came about.

It begins with Acrisius, king of Argos, who was warned by an oracle that any son born to his daughter would supplant him. She was Danäe, once Damkina the spouse of Ea the Goat-fish; and to prevent her conceiving, Acrisius immured her in a brazen tower. A useless precaution: hardly was she there than Zeus ravished her, in a shower of gold (the Babylonians would have said: by a commotion of the gods), or else it was her father's own brother, Proetus, King of Tiryns, who did so. Perseus was the result.

Danäe's tower was once the Perseus watch-tower that stood at the Canopic mouth of the Nile, not so distant from that on the island of Pharos where Proteus – who is the same as Proetus – has his home. The story is ancient, for both Perses, ancestor of the Persian kings, and Gilgamesh were conceived in the same way, both of them being thrown out of the tower when they were born, only to be caught up by an eagle and carried to a garden in the sky. Perseus himself, however, was put into a chest with his mother and thrown into the sea, much as Osiris was, floating at last to the island of Seriphos where they were fished out by Dikte ('net'). Dikte's brother Polydectes, who was king of the island, claimed Danäe for his own, but first had to get rid of Perseus to whom he gave the task of cutting off the head of the Gorgon Medusa, that petrifying lamia.

As soon as he had been armed with Athene's mirror-shield, the sickle and the winged sandals of Hermes, and Hades' helmet of invisibility, he flew to Libya where he cut off Medusa's head, having taken care to look at her meanwhile by reflection only. The head he put in his wallet. From her headless trunk sprang Pegasus the winged horse, Chrysaor the king of that part of Gaul where the Tarasque is now found, and the blood with which Asclepius could either kill or cure. He then visited Atlas, who was so inhospitable that he turned him to stone with one look from the Gorgon's head, and flew off to Joppa where a female sea-monster was ravaging the country. This was on account of Cassiopeia, who had rashly boasted that she was as beautiful as the Nereids; and to placate the jealous monster, her daughter Andromeda was just then chained naked to the rocks waiting to be eaten.

The monster was no match for Perseus, who then claimed Andromeda's hand from her father Cepheus. The wedding feast was in full swing when Cepheus's brother arrived, wanting Andromeda for himself. Another glance from the Gorgon's head put paid to him, together with Cepheus and Cassiopeia who are now constellated near Draco and the Pole Star. Perseus then returned to Argos where he restored his grandfather Acrisius, who had been dethroned by Proetus; to Seriphos, where he rescued his mother; and to Thessaly, where King Teutamas was celebrating the funeral games at the grave of his father. There Perseus competed in the discus throwing, and accidentally killed Acrisius as the oracle had said he would.

This complicated story has to do with two dragons, two incestuous uncles, a double kingdom, and presumably a year of two seasons, each with a human representative; and it has to do with their rivalry, and the claim to the succession which goes with marriage to the queen's daughter. The details of this system have long been forgotten, though about the killing of Acrisius the Etruscans have left us an interesting clue. They had a Perseus, whom they called *phersu*, who is shown in one tomb-painting as a masked figure at a funeral rite, where a human captive, tied with a rope, is about to be sacrificed to the dead man's shade. This fits in with both the Greek meaning of Perseus, 'the destroyer', and the Etruscan one which is at the origin of the Latin 'persona', the mask by which a dead man is known. It also throws light on the Gorgon's head, which some think to be the lineal descendant of Humbaba and all agree to have been nothing but a mask in the first place. Gorgon masks were by custom hung up in tombs; over ovens where bread or pottery was being baked, to deter the inquisitive; and they also marked the source of hot springs, for which Seriphos was celebrated. We can therefore imagine the Gorgon as a hot-blooded mélusine, the goddess of childbirth who in her demonic aspect must be stopped from carrying off both child and mother to the Isle of the Dead.

What this particular story means is another matter. It has come down to us pretty well intact in modern folklore, but with a few interesting changes – the second dragon, for instance, is killed underground, or under the water, the hero coming up to the surface on eagle-back; he puts the dragon's tongue, not its head, into his wallet, to give the lie to the interloper who claims his bride; and the second dragon is said to be mother to the first. This puts us forcibly in mind of the Babylonian creation epic, the underwater realm standing for Apsu or the Abyss, the dragon mother and son for Tiamat and Kingu, and the Gorgon's head or dragon's tongue for the splendour of kingship Marduk seized from Kingu. It looks, therefore, as if we are back at the spring equinox, and the ritual masquerade that was acted out at that time.

This masquerade has come down to us also, though in abbreviated form, either as a mummers' charade or a Lenten carnival. The full story of the charade starts with an old woman nursing a seven-months' child who grows up quickly, demands a bride and celebrates his wedding feast. During the feast an interloper molests the bride and kills the hero, over whom the bride weeps; but the hero is brought back to life, the interloper is overthrown and the marriage is royally consummated. The hero is sometimes called St George; his adversary is a Moor, foreigner or charcoal-burner, the bringer-

God of the hot springs at Bath. Romano-British.

back to life a doctor, and the main object of interest is the hobby or hooden horse, lineal descendant of the *drac*, who is ridden now by the hero, now by his rival.

The Slavs act out a play of this kind during the twelve days of Christmas, but with twelve men masked as animals, who stand for the twelve months and who bring with them the hosts of the dead roaring and battling in the air. In every house offerings are made to these spirits and to the maskers, while the inhabitants cry, bark and sing in joyful hubbub, and practise various forms of divination to see what destiny has written for the coming year. On Twelfth Night the masqueraders come for the last time, led by a man dressed as Master of all the animals. He is the year spirit himself, variously called Turon, or Bear, or Horse, who terrorizes young women and is given wine and honey to pacify his lusts. His followers, however, often take him to neighbouring villages and challenge them to combat. In Bulgaria these battles caused many deaths in the last century, which neither the law nor the Church took notice of, the corpses being buried outside the cemetery and without the last rites; a fitting sacrifice at the funeral games of the Old Year.

These festivals were once performed from Europe to China, and go back to the time of the Bronze Age at least. Some were celebrated in the winter, some in the spring, according to the time when the calendar began, and many of them in Europe have been shifted to coincide with Christian feasts. The festival of the Tarasque is one example, and it is only one of many French dragons that paraded the streets either on Ascension Day or on the Rogation Days leading up to it. This day of rejoicing marks the end of the Great Sacrifice, whose victim entered the dragon-mouth of Hell, harrowed its interior and then rose from the dead. Now he rises into Heaven, the sign of the birth of Man in God; and there he prepares the coming of the Holy Ghost that is to happen ten days later, at Pentecost – the second feast day of the Tarasque, and the celebration of the time when the apostles spoke in tongues, and were accused by unbelievers of being drunk.

The accusation is understandable, partly because of the ancient custom only to broach the vintage of the previous year at the start of the new one, partly because of a quite general equation made between the fermentation of alcoholic liquors and the birth of the spirit. It is no accident, therefore, that the pre-Christian god who looked after such matters was Dionysus, at once the year-god, the god of the vine and the resurrected spirit of Hades. His rites continue to this day in Thrace, practised by an initiatory corporation who pride themselves on bestowing fertility to the land and on curing sickness. The central figure of their ritual drama is the Kalogeros, or Beautiful Old One, his head covered by a pumpkin mask decorated with scraps of goatskin, who pursues young women with all the salacious vigour of a Turon. In his procession are a King and a Queen, a young Prince acting as cup-bearer and dispensing wine; the Old Woman with her seven-months' Dionysus-baby, who mimics sexual intercourse with a blacksmith or Moor; and a troop of young men who engage in a tug of war to decide the fortune of a coming year, and mimic the ploughing of a field. Seed is scattered there, and over the Kalogeros who is then 'murdered' and thrown into a water tank, only to come to life again and take the King's place in the

St Michael and the dragon. Norman.

ensuing dance. On May 21 the ritual course comes to an end with firewalking by those who have been born into the god through their devotion.

It might be thought that rites of this nature have little to do with dragons, in spite of the Kalogeros lusting after women, being killed and thrown as a sacrifice into the waters; or of the presence of a King whom the Kalogeros eventually supplants. But there is no doubt that the Kalogeros is none other than Dionysus, the Good Genius of the year whose other name is Hades, and whose life-blood is the wine that is so often drunk by the dragon-slayer. The question then is how this wine is made, and what the dragon has to do with it.

What must be one of the oldest accounts of this is the Hindu equivalent of the Perseus myth: the *Amrtamanthanam*, or Churning of Amrita. Amrita is the Deathless Drink, also called Soma; and Soma is the Dragon, or at least the liquor that jets from its decapitated trunk, like the sap that wells out from the trunk of a felled tree. The fate of Soma is to be poured into the womb of Agni the Fire; and this fire is made with firesticks whose name, *pramantha*, derives from that of churning. The symbolism of both, moreover, is explicitly based on sexual intercourse. With this in mind it will be seen that what the Hindus call the making of Soma is no other than what, for the Greeks, was the conception of Perseus.

The story goes, then, that the gods met at the top of Mount Meru, all of them afraid of death, which is the end, which is the year, which is Prajapati the progenitor. Vishnu, whose other name is Narayana – in Greek, Nereus – tells them that they can only avert the doom of perpetual hunger by calling in the anti-gods, the Danava – in Greek, the people of Danäe – and with their help churn Soma out of the primal waters. To do so they must first obtain the Vase of Ocean – the Brazen Cup of Nereus – from the Master of the Waters, and persuade the Tortoise King, himself often figured as a vase, to carry the weight of the operation. Vishnu then orders his serpent, Vasuki, to uproot Mandara the Churning Mountain, and loop itself around as a cable, so that the gods and the anti-gods can twirl the mountain to and fro in a cooperative tug of war. The serpent breathes out vapour, smoke, and poison; a storm of rain is unleashed, the ocean is worked into a fury, a rain of fire descends and is quenched, and every plant gives up its sap and resin to form a golden juice, the Butter of the Ocean and the ichor of the Golden Embryo. As the Soma is made, the Goddess of Fortune emerges from the waters together with a horse – Pegasus to the Greeks – and a divine jewel, the emblem of sovereignty that Vishnu takes for himself. Dhanvantara, the Hindu Asclepius, follows with the Soma cup, which the Danavas steal together with the Goddess.

So Vishnu dresses as a woman – one can remember how Susa No did the same in his calendar house – and seduces the Danava with his beauty to such effect that they give back what they have stolen, but not before Rahu their chief drinks down some of the brew. However, before it reaches his Adam's apple Vishnu cuts his head off with his discus (as Perseus did to his grandfather), the head then taking on an independent life as the Eclipse Demon, known in Europe as the Dragon's Head, or Ascending Node of the Moon. This brings on a general fight between gods and anti-gods, decided in the gods' favour after Indra (the Indian Marduk) kills the serpent Bala, who is Vishnu's other self. The gods then get drunk on Soma, and the New Year starts with happy auspices.

This ancient story curiously parallels the Babylonian creation epic in having the gods of a conquering people triumph over those of the aboriginal people, which are thereafter called anti-gods, and whose drama is then acted out by two ritual fraternities at the year's end. We have some indication of how these anti-gods were thought of, as far as the Danava are concerned: for their prince is called Kubera, Lord of Riches, and his people are the *yakshas* who live in a palace called the Bejewelled, and play music in their garden on Churning Mountain itself. 'Yaksha' means 'those who sacrifice', and the earliest Indian texts use this name to designate the Great Being from whom all gods sprout, as branches from the stem of a tree, whom they otherwise call Prajapati and Cosmic Pillar.

The top of this pillar reaches the Pole Star. But, because of the precession of the equinoxes, the Pole Star of the Danava was not our Polaris but a star in the tail of Draco – a constellation that has been identified as the Babylonian Tiamat, the Hindu Vasuki, and the Greek Ladon when it was still coiled in its Hesperidean tree. The Churning myth thus tells of the time when the location of the Pole was leaving Draco and approaching Polaris, and this meant that the abode of the gods also had to move. At this moment the yakshas lost their rank and became simple tree-demons or dryads, while the nagas – who are also tree-demons – took over their position.

Nagas are snakes, often pictured with a human body, who live at the top of the present Mountain of the Gods, Mount Meru, in a golden palace echoing with music, containing beautiful women, wish-fulfilling jewels, flowers and ambrosial refreshment. Their garden, which used to be the paradise of Varuna, is the place of incarnation, the dragon-haunted tree at its centre being hung with jewels in which the life of the Golden Embryo is hidden.

Is all this a delusion? And, if not, what kind of wish-fulfilment is involved? For we have chased the dragon through the Three Worlds – the firmament above, the firmament below, and the Earth between – and have now returned to our starting place. The dragon world seems to be formed in the manner of the Purse of Fortunatus – known to us as a Klein Bottle – whose singular property, as described by Lewis Carroll, is that 'Whatever is *inside* the Purse is *outside* it, and whatever is *outside* it, is *inside* it.'

We can give some kind of answer by enquiring once more into the making of the Golden Embryo. We are certainly dealing with a vision of

Dragon fight. Mochica, Peru.

28

Heavenly attendants. Chinese.

embryonic life here, as its name and the images associated with it confirm; but that it is golden allows us to return to alchemical ground, on which matter and spirit are mutually converted. We must therefore start with the Prime Matter, the dragon form of the Progenitor, and follow the rule of marrying it three times to its own reflection until the two of them conceive themselves anew as their own child. This reflection, of course, takes the form of a woman who is the *soror mystica* of the alchemist and indeed of any Hindu husband. For Hindu tradition says that a woman is successively the spouse of four partners: her first being Soma, not only as the life-giving sap but as the moon; her second the Gandharva, the divine musician on whose breath the spirits of unborn children are carried into the womb; her third Agni the Fire, the sexual appetite that heats the cauldron of birth; and her fourth the human husband, whose love-making merely provides the occasion for Soma, Agni and the Gandharva to perform the reproductive miracle that mercury, sulphur and the dragon accomplish between them when the alchemist husbands their energies.

The aim of the operator, in the rite of marriage as in that of alchemy, is to create something immortal in which he also has a part. This is why ritual texts always stress that a material operation can only be effective if it is simultaneously done in spirit; for if you do not, the Hindus say, you might as well push aside the brands and make oblation in the ashes. Their prescription for immortality in the flesh, which is one of the ancient Laws of Manu, is luckily much clearer than any given by the alchemists, whose Oedipus complexes had been humiliated by Original Sin: it states, quite simply, that 'the husband, after his wife has conceived, becomes an embryo and is born again of her; for that is the wifehood of a wife, that he is born again of her.'

Jonah. Franco-German Jewish.

This is the manner of immortality granted by the wish-fulfilling jewel, when it is plucked from the family tree whose dragon guardian embodies the spirit of the ancestors. It is for this reason that dragons are frequently the emblem of royalty, since the king is husband not only to his queen but to his realm, and has the dragons of earth and sky at his command. In this vein, the Chinese annals of the Han dynasty record that the birth of the emperor Hiao Wu was heralded by a dream in which his father saw a red fog descend from the clouds into the palace and enter the Exalted Fragrance Corridor. He awoke and sat in that corridor, which was full of a red fog that darkened doors and windows. The imperial harem was then summoned, and a cinnabar-coloured vapour arose and coiled itself dragon-wise in the rafters, above the imperial consort Wang. Ten days later the king dreamt again, of a divine woman who held up the sun in her outstretched hands and then gave it to the imperial consort, who swallowed it and duly became pregnant of the future emperor Hiao Wu.

Courtesies of this nature have very generally been paid to dragons in the East, where they are seldom harried to death as in the West. The Chinese have extended these courtesies so far that the emperor K'ung Kiah is said to have been presented by Heaven with a male and female dragon, which unfortunately died because he did not know how to feed them; though later a descendant of the emperor Yao learnt this art, and became the ancestor of the Imperial Dragon-rearers. The final courtesy, however, was paid in India when the Buddha was said to have lived as a naga king before his incarnation as a man; to have been bathed, as soon as born a man, by the naga king and queen, who later created a lotus leaf on which he might reveal himself; to have been sheltered during the storm of his illumination by the seven-headed naga, Mucilinda, who was the agent of that storm; and to have tamed a fire dragon by making it enter his alms-bowl, as one of his first deeds when Awakened.

The Buddha's example was followed by his disciples, who instead of killing nagas converted them to the faith and indeed made them its guardians. A fine instance is to be found in the story of the Zen priest Shinyu and the unknown goddess, protectress of the land, who invited him to climb to the top of Mount Hakusan and there worship her in her true form. He obeyed, and in answer to his prayers a nine-headed dragon arose from a small lake near the summit. Shinyu refused to acknowledge that a dragon could be her true form and so continued with his devotions until it had changed into the image of the eleven-faced Boddhisattva Kuanyin, whose lotus stalk and tame carp showed her to be the goddess of compassion and guardian of childbirth.

That the real form of a dragon can be a goddess should now cause us no surprise. Her lotus takes us back to the makara or Goat-fish who, as Ea, had his palace of birth in the Abyss; and its bud contains the Golden Embryo. The carp will be one of those who become dragons when they have made the ascent of those rapids called the Dragon's Gate on the headwaters of the Yellow River, and so attain Heaven. And the dragon is that serpent deity who, in the straightforward language of the Naassenes, 'contains within itself, like the horn of the one-horned bull, the beauty of all things; that pervades everything, like the water that flows out of Eden and divides into four sources'. The Naassenes said of this Eden that it was the brain, a conclusion also reached by the Hindus whose dragon-goddess goes by the name of Kundalini the Coiled. Her principal image is that of the lingam encircled by the yoni, and she sleeps in the lotus centre at the base of the spine. When she is aroused, she climbs up the spine between the interweaving channels of Ida and Pingala, the two heavenly rivers. Their final confluence is at the forehead, a place marked by a serpent-headed fillet in Egypt as well as India: and when Kundalini has arrived there, it is said that the scales of illusion fall from the inner eye and the Golden Embryo is seen as its pupil.

AB INSOMNI NON CVSTODITA DRACONE

'The dragon's nature is rough and fierce, yet he likes beautiful gems and the Stone of Darkness, and is fond of roasted swallows. He is afraid of iron, of the *wang* plant, of centipedes, of the leaves of the *lien* tree, and of five-coloured silk thread. Therefore those who have eaten swallows avoid crossing the water, and those who pray for rain use swallows; those who suppress water-calamity use iron, those who stir up the dragons to make rain use the *wang* plant, and those who offer to K'uh Yuen use leaves of the *lien* tree and coloured silk thread, wrapping dumplings in them which they throw into the river. Also when physicians use dragon's bones, they must know these particulars about the dragon's likings and hatreds.' (Li Shi-chen.)

(Dragon painting by Kano Mitsunobu on ceiling compartment, Shōkoku-ji, Kyoto, 16th century.)

The lintel above the doorway at Angkor Wat has carved upon it the sign for 'door', namely two makara-dragons with garlands for bodies. Above them is a door for the imagination, where he who runs may read, again framed by two makaras; and above that another pair, to make sure of the message. Cambodia is the land of makaras and nagas, of water-spirits and god-kings, of great reservoirs and irrigation ditches. And each reservoir

has its temple, where its divinity is worshipped in dragon form. For, as the Chinese say, 'Water is represented by means of dragons'. They also talk of the nine different young of the dragon, two of which account for the decoration of the Vietnamese pagoda roof: the *ch'i wen*, or mouth drums, which like to swallow and are placed at the end of the ridge-poles to swallow evil influences; and the *chao feng*, or dawn winds, at the eaves to disseminate good ones.

(Roof of Tay Phyong pagoda, near Say Son, Son Tay, Viet Nam, 15th century. Relief from Banteay Srei, Cambodia, 10th century.)

After the war in Heaven, 'the great dragon was cast out, that old serpent, called the Devil, and Satan, which deceiveth the whole world; he was cast down to Earth, and his angels were cast down with him' (*Revelation*, 12, 9). The dragon's mouth then became the door of Hell. But the *Book of Revelation* also says: 'Behold, I stand at the door,

and knock; if any man hear my voice, and open the door, I will come in to him and will sup with him, and he with me. To him that overcometh will I grant to sit with me on my throne, even as I also overcame, and am set down with my Father on his throne' (3, 20–21). (Souls thrust into the mouth of a monster, detail from a 13th-century window, Bourges Cathedral. A soul being rescued from the mouth of Hell, French enamel plaque, 14th century.)

The dragon, say the Chinese, has the eyes of a demon; and demons are luckily so idiotic that they have only to see a picture of themselves to flee in the opposite direction. The Gorgon also has the eyes of a demon, and thinks nothing of sticking her tongue out at the evil, the meddlesome and the grossly impertinent – her silent message is Keep Out Or Else.

However, if a grain of dust be in your eye, follow the custom of the old Italian peasantry: put your middle finger over the afflicted eye, close the other one, and say, 'I kiss the Gorgon's face'. The charm is powerful enough to draw a bone from the throat of a man or a mare. (Talisman from a Buddhist temple, South Korea. Gorgon painting on a Greek kylix.)

Ugrasena, rightful king of Mathura, was deposed by his son Kans; and Kans, a cruel and tyrannical ruler, was then told that the eighth son of his sister Rohini would cause his death. He had killed six of her children by the time Krishna, the eighth, was born: and to finish him off, Kans sent the dragon Aghasūr to waylay him and his fellow cowherds. The dragon's open mouth looked so like a mountain cave that Krishna and his friends walked right into it. Hardly had the dragon shut its mouth, however, than Krishna made himself so large that he burst its stomach, and everyone was able to escape unhurt.

Anyone who finds himself being swallowed by the gaping maw of Hell may draw some comfort from this story, and from the following list of words, which all derive from the same root: *giri*, Sanskrit for mountain; *gorge*, a ravine, also a throat; *gurges*, Latin for a gyrating whirlpool; *gargoyle*, a waterspout formed by the mouth of a dragon; *jargon*, from a word meaning to warble in the throat; and *giri* again, Sanskrit for speech, voice, praise, hymn. (Hell, detail of Last Judgment, fresco, Chiciora Church, Păusesti-Măglasi village, Romania, c. 1820. Snake demon swallows the cowherds, Indian watercolour, c. 1800.)

There are many dragons in France known to have a taste for young children, which they eat, and virgins, which they ravish. At least four of them are to be found in Provence: one at Aix, where it was burst asunder by St Margaret (numerous dinosaur eggs have also been found in the environs); one at Draguignan, where the mayor of the town has the right to have any of his godchildren christened 'Drac'; a third at Beaucaire, that specialized in catching nursing mothers and making them suckle baby dragons; and the most famous at Tarascon, tamed by St Martha, but first vanquished by Heracles when it bore the name of Tauriscus and guarded the entrance to the Celtic Tartarus.

Tartarus is a reduplication of Tar, the Egyptian name for the god of the underworld. The dragons on each side of the Tau cross exemplify the same duplication: indeed, the Christ Crucified, his mother on one side and St John on the other, is already in their conjoined belly. (Annual Tarasque festival procession, Tarascon. Greek ivory staff with Tau cross, 18th century.)

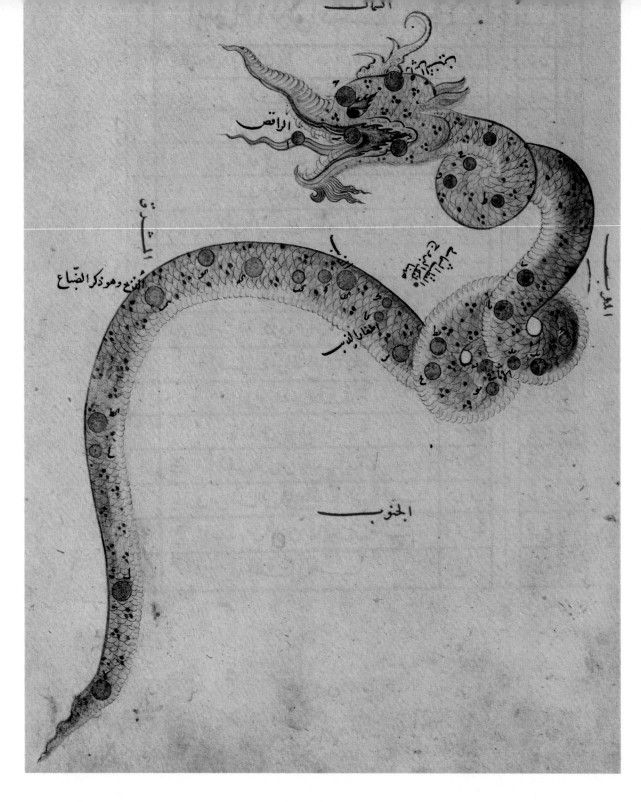

الراقص

الجنوب

When the Israelites were journeying through the Wilderness, from Mount Hor to the land of Edom, they were so plagued by hunger and thirst that they spoke against God, and Moses, for bringing them out of Egypt: and God sent fiery serpents to bite them for their presumption. Then Moses made a serpent of brass and set it on a pole, so that everyone who was bitten, when he looked upon it, should live.

The constellation of Draco has amongst its many titles that of *Monstrum mirabile et audax*. It is often figured as a combination of reptile and bird, like Belbelo's idiosyncratic horror, and is also set on a pole of a kind – the Pole of the ecliptic. There is no evidence, however, that the two are related, though they make a pretty pair. (Dragon from Sufi *Book of Constellations*, 12th century. Israelites smitten by a serpent, from *The Visconti Hours*, Italian, late 15th century.)

Phorcys was the Greek name for the sea-monster that was also the death-god – in Latin, Porcus or Orcus, from which comes our word *ogre*. Hence the swinish appearance of the fish that is here vomiting out Jonah upon the dry land.

The timely lance of Ruggiero is surprising a monster of this sort just before it can savour the pride of Angelica's reproachful nakedness. Ruggiero is the Italian form of the German Rüdiger, (which means Fame-Spear), and of the English Roger, whose name may vulgarly be used as a verb as occasion requires. (Jonah cast up by the whale, marble, Eastern Mediterranean, 3rd century. Angelica saved by Ruggiero, oil on canvas, by Jean-Auguste-Dominique Ingres, 1780–1867.)

It was the custom at Silene, in Libya, to sacrifice children to the dragon that lived in the swamp nearby. St George is said to have put a stop to this. In Palestine the children, who had to be first-born, were sacrificed to Moloch – a rite that the Old Testament calls 'making the children over to the King by fire', and which the ancient Hebrews also practised until the prophets persuaded them otherwise. It is this rite that the 12th chapter of the *Book of Revelation* alludes to: 'And there appeared a great wonder in Heaven; a woman clothed with the sun, and the moon under her feet, and upon her head a crown of twelve stars; and she, being great with child, cried, travailing in birth, and pained to be delivered . And there appeared another wonder in Heaven; and behold a great red dragon, having seven heads and ten horns, and seven crowns upon his head ... and the dragon stood before the woman which was ready to be delivered, for to devour her child as soon as it was born.'
(Child sacrificed to the dragon, detail from Altarpiece of St George, Valencia, c. 1400. Dragon persecuting woman clothed with the sun, detail from Altarpiece of the Apocalypse, German, attributed to Meister Bertram, 14th century.)

49

'"I am a Hebrew," he cries—and then – "I fear the Lord the God of Heaven who hath made the sea and the dry land!" Fear him, O Jonah? Aye, well mightest thou fear the Lord God *then*! ... But all in vain; the indignant gale howls louder; then, with one hand raised invokingly to God, with the other [the mariners] not unreluctantly lay hold of Jonah.

'And now behold Jonah taken up as an anchor and dropped into the sea; when instantly an oily calmness floats out from the east, and the sea is still, as Jonah is carried down the gale with him, leaving smooth water behind. He goes down in the whirling heart of such a masterless commotion that he scarcely heeds the moment when he drops seething into the yawning jaws awaiting him; and the whale shoots-to all his ivory teeth, like so many white bolts, upon his prison.' (Herman Melville: *Moby Dick*.)

The Hebrews abominated the sea. The Greeks, though knowing what it could do to ships, called its eldest son Nereus, 'who is true and tells no lies'. They said also that Nereus had fifty daughters, gracious, rosy-armed and lovely of shape: amongst them were Sao the Rescuer, Erato the Desirous, Hipponoë the One Wise as a Horse, Thetis the Disposer, and Amphitrite 'who calms the waves upon the misty sea and the blasts of raging winds'.

(Nereid riding dragon, cover of a Hellenistic silver bowl. Jonah swallowed by the whale, detail of mosaic floor, Apuleia Cathedral, 4th century AD.)

St Margaret, cast in durance vile by a wicked pagan, burst open the dragon that swallowed her by making the sign of the Cross, and her happy delivery turned her into the patron saint of childbirth. When

she and the dragon combine, as
may be said to have happened in
the Mughal miniature, they are seen
to be the goddess who gives birth to
everything – to the eater and the
eaten alike.

(St Margaret emerging from the
dragon, Book of Hours, north
France, 15th century. Composite
monster, Mughal miniature, late
17th century.)

' "Flying dragon in the heavens. It furthers one to see the great man." What does this signify?

'The Master said: Things that accord in tone vibrate together. Things that have affinity in their inmost natures seek one another. Water flows to what is wet, fire turns to what is dry. Clouds follow the dragon, wind follows the tiger. Thus the sage rises, and all creatures follow him with their eyes. What is born of Heaven feels related to what is above. What is born of Earth feels related to what is below. Each follows its kind.' (Commentary on the hexagram ch'ien, *Book of Changes,* translated by R. Wilhelm.) (Popular dragon woodcut, Tibet.)

Dragon boats are normally reserved for those who indulge in pillage, like the Vikings; who make it rain, like Chinese emperors; who bear with them a full complement of good news, like Noah in his ark; or who go to the other world.

These conditions must have applied to the Buddhist monk Gishō, who came to China in the 7th century and returned to Korea carrying with him the teachings of the Kegon sect. During his stay a Chinese girl fell in love with him: and as he took ship once more she threw herself into the sea, turning into a dragon that bore his ship safely to its destination.

Journeys to the other world may nowadays be undertaken as a pleasure trip, provided the sightseer has a round ticket.
(Detail of handscroll attributed to Enichi-bo-Jonin: *Kegonshu Soshi eden*, Japan, 13th century. Modern dragon boat, Japan.)

'When rain is to be expected, the dragons scream and their voices are like the sound made by striking copper basins. Their saliva can produce all kinds of perfumes. Their breath becomes clouds, and they avail themselves of the clouds to cover

their bodies. At the present day, on rivers and lakes, there are some-times people who see one claw and the tail, but the head is not to be seen. In summer, after the fourth month, the dragons divide the regions amongst themselves and each of them has his territory. This is the reason why within a distance of a couple of acres there may be quite different weather: rain and a clear sky. Further, there are often heavy rains, and those who speak about these rains say: "Fine moistening rain is heavenly rain, violent rain is dragon rain."' (Wang Fu.)

(Dragon, detail of a painting attributed to Nonomura Sotatsu, Japan, 17th century.)

The Chinese emperor had as his badge the Dragon King, who issues his commands by moving in all four directions simultaneously. The fifth direction is called the Centre, where he remains; hence he has five claws. Local and subsidiary dragons are allowed no more than four.

The first emperor to assume a dragon form was Fu Hsi, before history began, who put the Great Waters into order by digging dykes, canals and irrigation ditches, and so tamed the Yellow River. It is said that Heracles did the same to the Hydra, by dyking parts of the unfathomable swamps near the town of Lerna. The Hydra had nine heads, one of them golden and immortal, which Heracles struck off after the others and buried, still hissing, beneath a rock. This happened when the sun was in Cancer, and the spirits of the dead return to Earth to be reincarnated. What it means for a woman to wear the Hydra on her breast these days is something for any Heracles worth his name to labour on.

(Art Nouveau corsage ornament by Réné Lalique, 1860–1945. Imperial badge, Chinese, 18th century.)

The naga lord lives in a happy land filled with troops of lively girls, gladdened constantly by their sports and by music, dancing and feasts. According to the Samyuktavadana Sutra, however, 'he has to endure three kinds of suffering: his delicious food turns into toads as soon as he takes it into his mouth; his beautiful women, as well as himself, change into serpents when he tries to embrace them; on his back he has scales lying in a reverse direction, and when sand and pebbles enter between them, he suffers pains which pierce his heart. Therefore do not envy him.'

He also owns the most precious of jewels, which the Chinese call 'the pearl that grants all desires', saying

that it is certain to be found in a pool nine layers deep under the chin of a horse-dragon. This pearl controls the phases of the moon; the ebb and flow of the tide; rain, thunder and lightning; and the course of birth, death, and rebirth. Such pearls are sometimes spat out by dragons, and may be used to illuminate a whole house (or a whole man); and if kept in the mouth, it is as though you were drinking the finest wine.

(Naga sculpture from the Konarak Sun Temple, India, 13th century. Ivory dragons fighting for the crystal ball, China, 19th century.)

Kadru, 'Chalice of Immortality', and Vinata, 'She before whom Knowledge bows' were the wives of Kasyapa the sage. Kadru laid a thousand eggs which, after five hundred years, hatched into snakes; Vinata but two, the first hatching half-formed (it is the Dawn) and the second after another five hundred years as Garuda.

Vinata became Kadru's slave after betting that the sun's horses were white, and Kadru had won by a dirty trick. To win Vinata's freedom, Garuda agreed to steal the *amrita* of the gods, which he did by flying through the spokes of the sun-wheel, defeating the naga guardians, and evading Indra's thunderbolt. He brought the *amrita* to the thousand snakes, who went to bathe themselves before partaking of

the sacred substance: so that Indra had ample time to steal it back from them.

Garuda means 'Wings of Speech'; he embodies the Three Vedas, and carries Vishnu, Lord of the Sacrifice, upon his back. He is brilliant, virile, lustful, terrifying, takes what shapes he pleases, can stop the triple world from turning by the wind of his wings, and is the enemy of the Ever-Moving, the nagas who are the cycles of time. 'This bird beautiful of wing, is courage itself made into a bird.'
(Garuda, from the ceiling of Chiwong Gompa in the Himalayas, Nepal.)

Carved wooden crook. Collection Francis Huxley.

Themes

where it may be called either the Evening or the Morning Star, according to whether the dragon is about to imprison the light, or the light is about to be born from the dragon. The sun, who as the dragon's child has its own voracious appetite, then becomes the dragon-slayer, and will be found to eat tomorrow's dragons with the same regularity that it has eaten yesterday's. In this rôle it is often figured by the eagle – the Indian Garuda – which carries prayers and promises up to the sky, blessings and ordinances down to the earth, and a thunderbolt when it is angry.

Having this bird's eye view, the mind then appoints itself to be the World Architect, and sets about squaring the circle and cubing the sphere. Its first instruments are the posts that it sets up at the four corners of the world, by which it can give itself directions from its place at the centre underneath the Pole Star. These five then become the house-posts on which the canopy of the heavens is spread, and the props separating the upper firmament from the lower.

So a house is formed, in the very body of the dragon, with the hearth fire answering to the sun above; and a city may be built on the same plan, its ruler calling himself Lord of the World. The dragon is then banished to the dungeons below, or to the outer walls, to defend the mighty fortress of the god.

this page:

The Heavenly Jerusalem, from *Commentary on the Apocalypse of St John* by Beatus of Liebana, produced at Gerona, *c*.975. Gerona Cathedral Library.

Engraving from Principio Fabrizi: *Delle allusioni, imprese et emblemi*, Rome, 1588.

facing page:

The Great Turtle. A.P. Maudslay: *Biologia Centrali-Americana*, 1889–1902.

Detail of the restored Huaca del Dragón at Chanchán, Chimú culture.

Doorway with Garuda, Nepal.

Gate of Kilmainham Jail, Dublin.

Dragon palace

The dragon has been given many titles – the Wise, the Terrible, the Magnificent, the Abominable, the Embracer, the Overseer, the Lord of the World. But when, before time began, it had not yet differentiated its being from its non-being, its light from its darkness, its sky from its earth, it can hardly be called by a more fitting name than *tad ekam*,

Sanskrit for That One. For much the same reasons, Freud talked of the *id* when confronted by the apparently unorganized parts of the human psychic apparatus. Jung called this the collective unconscious, when the id showed him that it had a mind of its own.

This first stirring of the mind is known as the dragon's precious stone, or wish-fulfilling jewel. At the beginning it finds itself placed right in the dragon's jaws,

The way in is the way out

It is often difficult to know whether someone who is in the dragon's jaws is coming or going since, like Omar Khayyám visiting doctor and saint, he evermore comes out by the same door where in he went. What is certain, however, is that any passenger who has embarked aboard the dragon must endure the kind of voyage that Jonah made from the time he was thrown to the whale until he was vomited up again on the dry land; or that Jason took from Argos to Colchis, where he was to rescue the Golden Fleece from its serpent guardian.

The charnel house within the dragon's belly is called Hell. Its bad reputation has been only partly saved by the exploit of St Margaret, that pearl amongst women, who broke its belly open by making the sign of the Cross and so became the patroness of childbirth. In this she did but follow the example of the Christ, who used the sign of Jonah to foretell that he would be three days and three nights in the heart of the earth; while Jonah must have used the sign of Oannes the Babylonian fish-god, also called Ea, who knew everything and emerged from the Erythrean Sea to inform mankind accordingly.

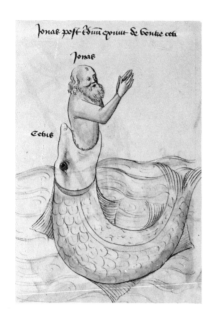

facing page:

Aztec stone rattlesnake pendant, its jaws enclosing a human head. University Museum of Archaeology and Ethnology, Cambridge.

Two men appearing from the mouth of a snake. Watercolour, Turkestan, 19th century. The Nasli M. Heeramaneck Collection, Gift of Joan Palevsky, Los Angeles County Museum of Art.

11th-century carved wood panel from Bjarnastahalid, Skagafjördur. National Museum of Iceland, Reykjavik.

Red-figure vase-painting of Jason spewed up by the dragon, c.475 BC. Museo Etrusco Gregoriano, Vatican, Rome.

this page:

Jonah coming out of the whale, from 14th-century Latin Bible. Bibliothèque Nationale, Paris, Ms. 5520 Lat. 512, f.34.

St Margaret, from a manuscript executed in northern France at the end of the 13th century. Bibliothèque Nationale, Paris, Ms. N.a.fr. 16521, f.100.

Maiden emerging from dragon. 14th-century statue. Northern France.

Stylized plumed serpent frieze on façade of the Temple at Tula, Mexico.

Jonah and the whale. Relief carving on sarcophagus. Museo Christiano Lateranense, Rome.

One in a circle

The ancients held that the most perfect shape was a circle, and that when a circle becomes a sphere it may be called an egg. Some held that the world itself was once an egg floating upon the bosom of the first waters, until there hatched out the Majesty of All Things (called Eros by the Orphics) who broke the shell in two and so formed the upper and the lower firmaments. The upper firmament is the origin of the sweet waters, in which children are baptized when they are born; though a pinch of salt is added to the font in memory of

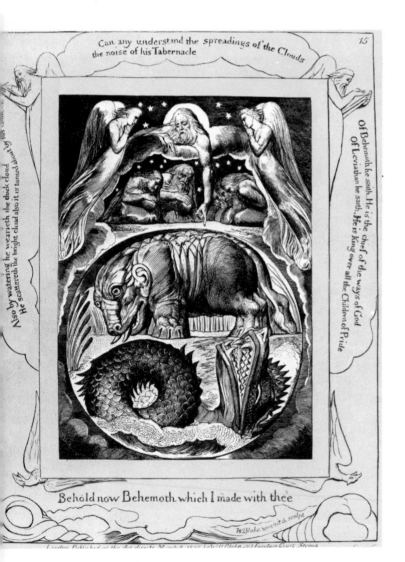

the Mistress of Salt Waters, whose flood is now shut up with doors after it had issued forth as if out of the womb; and whose son Leviathan will be eaten by the faithful on Judgment Day.

The Hindus give the newborn Majesty the name of Krishna, one of whose feats was to dance upon the head of Kaliya, the serpent of the whirlpool, until its four wives came to beg for mercy. How the Majesty of the Olmecs subdued the Feathered Serpent is not known, nor what he was called. He has, however, obviously obeyed William Blake's injunction to God:

If you have formed a circle to go into,
Go into it yourself and see how you
would do.

Leviathan. Ambrosian Bible. Ulm, southern Germany, 1236–38. Biblioteca Ambrosiana, Milan, B.32 inf. fol.136r.

'Behold now Behemoth'. Engraving by William Blake, pl.15 in *Book of Job*. British Museum, London.

70

Sol and Luna enthroned on their royal
egg, gilded by the fertilizing serpent.
Engraving from Joannes Daniel Mylius:
Philosophia Reformata, 1622.

The wives of the vanquished snake
Kaliya plead with Vishnu. 18th-century
Guler manuscript. Victoria and Albert
Museum, London.

Christ bruising the serpent's head.
Sculpture on font in the Church of
St Chad, Kirkby.

Drawing of Monument 19 from La
Venta, from Peter David Joralemon:
A Study of Olmec Iconography; studies in
Pre-Columbian Art and Archaeology No.
7, Dumbarton Oaks, Washington D.C.
1971.

The seductress in the waters

The dragon's daughters are famed for their beauty, their wisdom, their singing and their dancing, and other erotic accomplishments. They may be encountered wherever water bubbles out of the earth; they also ride the white horses of the sea, which from time to time throws up a sweetly cleft shell upon the shore.

It should not be forgotten, however, that they remain dragon from the hips down, and that it is difficult to enjoy them in the usual way without being drowned, or torn apart by Scylla the Render. However, they will agree to marry mortal men, sometimes out of love, sometimes because they have been manfully overpowered; and they stay faithful for as long as their bad is rhythmically taken along with their good, and they are not blamed for their peculiar relations.

facing page:

Champa sculpture of makara holding two women in its jaws. Musée Guimet, Paris.

4th-century terra-cotta floor-tile. Buddhist. Srinagar Museum.

Detail from frieze of Marriage of Poseidon and Amphitrite on an altar from the Temple of Neptune, Rome. Staatliche Antikensammlungen und Glyptothek, Munich.

this page:

Crab and Scylla on a silver coin from Agrigento, Sicily, c. 420–415 BC. Museo Archeologico Nazionale, Agrigento.

Fol.192v. from the Book of Durrow, 7th century. Trinity College Library, Dublin.

The weather-maker

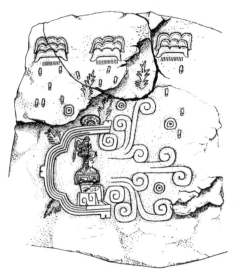

The hurricane is named after Huracan, the dragon of the Caribbean who is also responsible for earthquakes. He has two arms, the one crooked up and the other down, to show that he goes spinning; and he usually has but one leg, which is all he needs when walking about as a tornado.

His Olmec brother takes the form of a man, who is not only sitting on the sign for spin but holds a bar with the same sign in his hands. He lives in Dragon-mouth Cave – the dragon's eye with its flaming eyebrows and an X for a pupil is just above him – out of which comes a mist-laden breath that calls down the rain. The feathery objects are plants, and the four sets of concentric circles are the signs for precious jade-water.

The weather-maker prefers to make his home in the belly of the mountains, where he may rush down the valleys and sweep up again in giant swirls. The Norwegians long ago set him to guard the gables of their churches against the elements, or as though the church itself was where the winds are born: and Islam hints at their function there, by having Muhammad's magic steed mount to Heaven by virtue of dragon's breath.

Dormiens vigilat. Engraving from Principio Fabrizi: *Delle allusioni, imprese et emblemi*, Rome, 1588.

Drawing of relief I from Chalcatzingo, after Michael D. Coe: *The Jaguar's Children: Pre-Classic Central Mexico*; The Museum of Primitive Art, New York 1965, fig.10.

Muhammad meets the prophet Abraham in Heaven. Apocalypse of Muhammad, Turkish manuscript. Bibliothèque Nationale, Paris, Ms. Sup. turc. 190 fol.28v.

Tornado in the United States, June 1968.

Wood dragon-carving on roof of Lom
Stave church, Norway.

Engraving by J.M.W. Turner. Collection
Francis Huxley.

Mysterious principles of the Blue Bag

Chinese maps are drawn with the south at the top. This is the direction you should face in order to comprehend the landscape: then the Green Dragon of the east is at your left hand, which is Yang, and the White Tiger of autumn is at your right, which is Yin. In front of you the sun will be at its zenith, and behind you there is the darkness of winter.

A mountain is Yang also, and so are large rocks, steep waterfalls, age-old pines. It is most Yang on its sunny side, and Yin in its own shadow; and Yin also comprises what is low, cavernous, in a valley, and boggy. If you are looking for a place to build a house, or bury your ancestors, you should therefore go to a south-facing slope, with the Green Dragon animating the landscape to your left, and the White Tiger prowling harmlessly (because harmoniously) to your right, and these two should enclose the site as if by the crook of an elbow. At your front there should be a body of water.

The physiognomy of a landscape is so complex that you cannot be sure of your ground without the help of a *feng-shui* diviner, who understands how every part of it is animated by breath. *Feng-shui*, wind and water, bespeaks the two most obvious constituents of dragon's breath; for the others the diviner needs a magnetic compass. This may have as many as thirty-eight concentric rings about the needle, each divided into one of the ideal measures

of space and time. Using this, the diviner takes sights on the veins of the dragon, which are the raised features of the landscape, noting the watercourses, the trees, rocks, and branching of valleys; and should they fall upon an auspicious setting, a house built there will make its owner prosperous, and ancestors buried in that place will bless their descendants.

Such a site is called the Dragon's Head, and it should be consecrated with offerings in the shape of a dragon; and when the house is built, the dragon is invited to make its abode in a special niche. A garden may also be laid out, a private world of yin-and-yangeries where the dragon may lovingly disport; and it can further be honoured with figures of itself, to remind it of its good fortune.

Feng-shui diviners are themselves credited with dragonish powers, not only because they can discern dragons but because they can influence them according to the principles of the Blue Bag, which is their name for the universe. They are largely responsible for the finest use of the landscape the world knows, for the same reasons that Chinese landscape painting has the oldest and richest tradition of its kind.

facing page:

View of the Great Wall, Chihli Province, China. Ernst Boerschmann: *Picturesque China*, pl.2.

Geomantic diagram from Chinese text. Courtesy Stephan Feuchtwang.

Chinese landscape depicted in geomantic diagram, top right.

Tomb in China. Ernst Boerschmann: *Picturesque China*, pl.207.

this page:

Part IV of Nine Dragon Scroll by Ch'en Jung. Sung dynasty painting, mid-13th century. Courtesy Museum of Fine Arts, Boston, Francis Gardner Curtis Fund.

Detail from the scroll *The Metamorphosis of Heavenly Beings* by Li Kung-lin (c.1040–60). British Museum, London.

Secret ceremony to consecrate a temple, Taiwan.

Slaying the dragon

How best to kill dragons has been the subject of many a debate. The method most favoured by chivalry is to engage it in battle when on horseback, and to so manage the lance that it slides effort-lessly between the dragon's jaws. Engagements of this kind are usually carried out in spring, when young men's fancies meet with the approbation of nature.

The same deed was accomplished in Egypt when the Horus boat of the sun had to sail over the Apophis serpent of the dead season. Apophis is killed by Set, who is more famous for his murder of Osiris: which we could interpret by saying that Apophis is Osiris' alter ego.

Heracles managed the same feat, though he is not known ever to have mounted a horse, ridden in a chariot like Marduk, or sailed in anything but the Brazen Cup of the night sun. He is about to cut out the monster's tongue, which will not only demasculinize it but give him the ability to understand the language of the birds. St Michael is about to do the same to Satan, early identified with the Crooked Serpent of the Old Testament; though he is of course an archangel, and so must already know God's secret language.

Perseus has no steed either, when killing the Gorgon: as he is wearing the helmet of invisibility lent him by Hades, he does not need speed to catch her by surprise. It is she, in any case, who gives birth to a horse when her head is cut off (this is why she can be pictured as a centaur), and this horse will be ridden by another hero to kill the Chimera.

The French later knew this horse as Bayart, and its owner or parent as the ogre Renouart who lived on the island of Volcano with two dragons for company. Maugis the magician, when questing for this horse, first dressed himself to look just like this ogre, who was thus easily put into a trance-like sleep; after which he clobbered the two dragons into sub-mission, his disguise protecting him from their flames, and found Bayart more than willing to leave his golden but waterless stable.

facing page:

Seth killing Apophis, from the Book of
the Dead of Lady Gheritwebeshet.
Papyrus, Egypt, 21st dynasty (1085–950
BC). Cairo Museum.

Heracles and the Sea-Monster. Greek
black-figure vase-painting. Attica.

St Michael and the Dragon on sculptured slab at St Nicholas, Ipswich.

this page:

Perseus decapitating Medusa. Detail of
neck of Boeotian pithos, 7th century BC.
Musée du Louvre, Paris.

Maugis fights the dragon and tames the
horse Bayart. From *Renaud de
Montauban*, 15th-century manuscript.
Bibliothèque de l'Arsenal, Paris.

Carpaccio: *St George Killing the Dragon.*
S. Giorgio, Venice.

The first parents

The dragon is not killed, say the alchemists, unless by a brother and a sister, who are the sun and moon. There are actually three dragons involved in the illustration: Python, who attempted to ravish the mother of the sun and moon, and may well have succeeded; Orion, accused by Apollo of ravishing one of his sister Artemis's handmaids; and the one formed out of the jealous attachment between brother and sister, which gives rise to recriminations of adultery on the one hand and suspicions of incest on the other.

The Trobrianders show a fine understanding of the intimate way that a woman harbours a dragon, and hints at the fate of any bird that tries to make its nest there. The alchemists say of this dragon that it kills its wife at the time she kills it; both are then perfused with the one blood, and must be buried. From their corruption then arises the tree of life, the regenerated dragon climbing up into the branches which bear a not accidental likeness to the antlers of the stag couched at the tree's foot. All is then set for the Temptation and the expulsion of our first parents from the garden of generation.

This same scene has an eagle figured underneath the stag. This is the thunderbird, messenger of Zeus (or however the High God is called), who brings the barren season to an end by laying it flat on its back and opening its jaws with its

beak. The immediate result of this encounter is that Mother Nature, who as Lilith was Adam's first companion, no longer has to feed the serpents in her bosom but gives abundantly of her milk. This milk the alchemists called 'of Magnesia', which means that it is a magnetic fluid: it is particularly active in spring, when it may be extracted from the dew, and by the time autumn comes it has ripened the vintage, and the wine made from it is drunk to celebrate the beginning of the coming year. The beginning of this cycle was described by Chaucer:

Whan that Aprille with his shoures sote
The droghte of March hath perced to the rote,
And bathed every veyne in swich licuor,
Of which vertu engendred is the flour;
Whan Zephirus eek with his swete breeth
Inspired hath in every holt and heeth
The tendre croppes, and the yonge sonne
Hath in the Ram his halfe cours y-ronne,
And smale fowle maken melodie
That slepen al the night with open yë,
(So priketh hem nature in hyr corages):
Then longen folk to goon on pilgrimages...

This was also the time when the Vikings longed to go a-raiding: and the dragon heads on the prows of their long ships speak plainly of the appetites stirred up by the spring, which for them included slaughter, pillage and rape.

facing page:

Sun and Moon killing dragon. From Michael Maierus: *Atalanta fugiens*, 1617.

De Secretis Naturae. From Michael Maierus: *Atalanta fugiens*, 1617.

Woodcut from Basilius Valentinus: *Occulta Philosophia*, 1613.

Detail of The Third Day of Creation. Manuscript of St Ambrose, *Hexaëmeron*, Regensburg, c.1170. Bayerische Staatsbibliothek, Munich. Ms. Clm. 14399, f.40r.

Painted wooden dance shield from the Trobriand Islands. British Museum, London.

this page:

Adam and Eve and the Serpent in the Tree of Knowledge. Powder flask with ivory carving. German, 16th century. Victoria and Albert Museum, London.

Post in the form of an animal head, found in the ship-burial at Oseberg, south Norway. Universiteets Oldsaksamling, Oslo.

Maiden-snakes in a vineyard. Detail of black-figure vase-painting on a Greek cylix. Staatliche Antikensammlungen und Glyptothek, Munich.

Wood carving of eagle attacking dragon. Collection Francis Huxley.

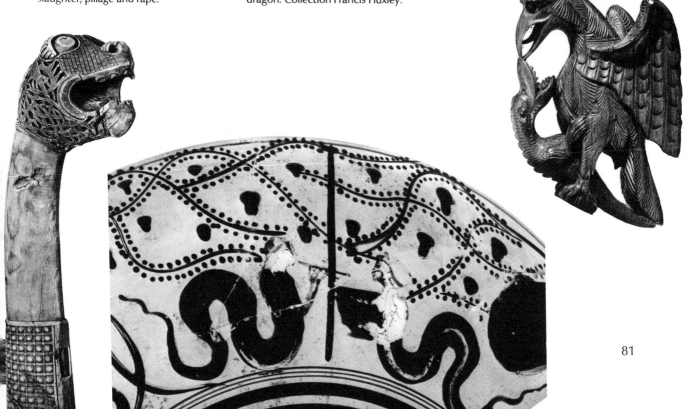

Wrestling with the dragon

Conchobar of Ireland had a divine and a human father, and he was born at the winter solstice with a water-worm, or baby dragon, clutched in each fist as evidence of the fact. Heracles likewise had two fathers; he was in addition one of twins, and he strangled two serpents on the anniversary of his birth, which was at midnight at the winter solstice (though some say at the spring equinox). A Sumerian hero, whose name is not known, obviously performed the same feat while standing between two lionesses, whose upraised tails discover the place from which heroes of this calibre are born.

Heracles had two proper encounters with river dragons: one with Achelous, whom he bested in a fight for the hand of Deianira; the other with Ladon, then guarding the apple-tree of the Hesperides. On his defeat Ladon was translated into the sky as the constellation Serpens, and put into the charge of Ophiuchus, the Serpent Holder. Ophiuchus was also known as Asclepius, who could bring the dead back to life, and Ladon became his curative serpent; but Asclepius himself is sometimes pictured as a serpent, being like Heracles the child of a human and a divine father.

Serpens is called Al Hayyah by the Arabs, a name which some like to think is related to Hawwah, as Eve the Mother of all living is called in Hebrew. Whether this is so or not, the child of a god and a mortal is born only by making the jaws of its prison gape; and at this moment the dead also emerge, to be reborn.

The Chinese seem to have found another way to subjugate the dragon, but just what it is being tempted with to open its mouth is hard to decipher. The plant of immortality, perhaps. As for Krishna, he just danced on the creature's head.

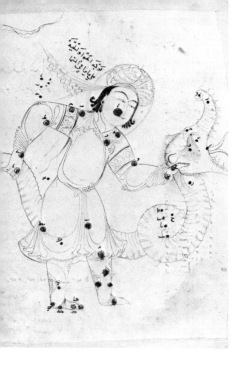

facing page:

Infant Heracles strangles two snakes.
Roman bronze, Imperial period. British
Museum, London.

Infant Heracles strangling snake. Greek
coin, 4th century BC. British Museum,
London.

Relief carving of man holding two
snakes. Steatite bowl, Sumerian, c.2700
BC, from Khafajah, central Iran. British
Museum, London.

Heracles wrestling Achelous. Detail of
red-figure stamnos painting by Oltos.
British Museum, London.

this page:

Constellation from a copy of the *Book of
Fixed Stars* by 'Umar as-Sūfi, illustrated in
Mosul, 13th century. British Museum,
London, Ms. Or. 5323, f.24v.

Shaman and dragon. Earthenware relief
from a Funerary Stove Model, Sian-fu,
Shensi Province, China. Han dynasty
(206 BC–220 AD). The Cleveland Museum
of Art, Charles W. Harkness Fund.

Detail of an architrave on the Great
Stupa, Sanchi.

Krishna dancing on Kaliya. Copper
statue, South India, Chola Period,
10–11th century. Collection Mr and
Mrs John D. Rockefeller 3rd.

83

One in two, and two in one

There are several ways of marrying a human being to a serpent. The commonest is to join the top of the one to the bottom of the other, as the Chinese arranged for their first emperor, Fu Hsi, and his consort Nu Kua. The Dogon of Africa, who have a similar convention, say that the First Ancestor is himself bisexual, being masculine at the head and feminine in the body, his consort having things the other way round. What the Greeks thought about these matters is obscure, though they sometimes pictured their First Gods as having two tails, each differently ornamented and coupling with its twin.

The Kwakiutl of Canada got over the difficulty by having one snake with two heads, joined in the middle by an admonitory head: this was worn as a belt by warriors, to decide the outcome between life and death. The Aztecs used the same motif in their figure of Coatlicue the snake-goddess and earth-mother, whose head is formed by those of two opposed serpents, and who bears on her breast the hearts of two sacrificed victims between two pairs of severed hands. The buckle on her belt is a skull, counter-image of her son Huitzilopochtli, god of war and personification of the sun.

The Christian tradition has its own version of this ancestral bisexuality, in which Lucifer appears as a human-headed serpent; and since he is Eve's reflection, reasons of symmetry have made some artists point broadly to Adam's association with the Tree. A later variation on this theme shows the blindfolded Eros announcing the contention of love with the opposed voices of two trumpets, rather than a forked tongue; the contestants making the kind of music most suitable to their generative abilities. What all this has to do with the Fall is gnomically expressed by Simone Weill: It is the punishment of the crime to have nourished love with imagination.

Rubbing from stone bas-reliefs on tomb of Wu Liang near Chia Hsiang Hsien.

Typhon, detail of a Greek red-figure vase-painting. Staatliche Antiken-sammlungen und Glyptothek, Munich.

Eros. Icon, 1825. Byzantine Museum, Athens.

The Sisiutl. Design by Russell Smith, Kwakiutl Tribe. British Columbia.

Aztec statue of Coatlicue. Museo Nacional de Antropologia, Mexico.

Jacopo della Quercia: *Original Sin* portal, San Petronio, Bologna.

Reptilian creature. Rendering by Felipe
Dávalos of painting I–C in Oxtotitlan
Cave. From David C. Grove: *The Olmec
Paintings of Oxtotitlan Cave, Guerrero,
Mexico*; Studies in Pre-Columbian Art
and Archaeology No. 6, Dumbarton
Oaks, Washington D.C. 1970.

Greek bronze Chimera. Archaeological
Museum, Florence.

Large winged Worm. Norman tym-
panum of chapel at Netherton,
Herefordshire.

Monstrum horrendum, informe, ingens

A frightful monster, ill-formed, huge, should all the same be made of recognizable parts if it wishes to pass as a dragon. The Olmecs of Mexico had a fancy for rattlesnakes, to which they added the eyebrows of a jaguar and a reminiscence of feathers. The Cham monster is something like an elephant, and something like a crocodile, with a hint of lion; it wears something else's horns, and if its ears are mistaken for tropical flowers no one is the loser. The Greeks once pictured the seasons by means of a thing 'more terrible than Woordes and of that which Men call a Chimera', as Lewis Carroll punningly said; but whether the Normans wished their monster to do anything but give people the creeps is debatable.

The Chinese said that a dragon was nine in one: it should have the horns of a stag, the head of a camel, the eyes of a demon, the neck of a snake, the belly of a clam, the scales of a carp, the claws of an eagle, the feet of a tiger, and the ears of a cow; also that it should have a large lump on the top of its head, without which it could not fly, and that the scales under its throat point in the wrong direction. The naga lord of Angkor Wat is a simpler monster, whose seven heads bear a studied resemblance to that of the black buffalo ridden by Yama, king of the dead in India: its keeper understandably needs seven pairs of hands to control it, one for each planetary sphere.

Makara. Cham sculpture, 13th century. Musée Guimet, Paris.

Naga sculpture at the end of a balustrade, Preah Khan, Angkor.

Making the world go round

'The derisive remark was once made against psychoanalysis', said the psychoanalyst Ferenczi, 'that the unconscious sees a penis in every convex object and a vagina or anus in every concave one. I find that this sentence well characterizes the facts.' This agreeable truism partly accounts for the way that the gods and anti-gods roped themselves to Churning Mountain by means of the World Serpent, and agitated it to and fro until the ocean of the Abyss conceived the solar system. The Tupinamba of Brazil went through much the same motions when clubbing an enemy to death, whose flesh was to provide a fertilizing meal to the assembled throng: the rope he was tied by was called *mussurana*, after a cannibalistic snake of that name, and he comforted himself by thinking that the manner of his death would let him be born into the best of afterworlds.

Europeans put this snake into the sky as Draco, whose principal coil lies around the Ecliptic Pole (here seemingly figured by Heracles). The Pole Star was once in Draco's tail, till the polar axis wandered off in the direction of our present Polaris; and since the ancients did not know if it would continue in a circle, or reverse upon its tracks, they used the image of a reciprocal churning to cover both eventualities.

The axial point of this motion is rendered in China by the form of the T'ai Chi, circular compendium of the Yin and Yang; or by the dragon pearl, often signed by a spiral. That the dragon is itself the pole which it goes around is no secret, and by now it should also be clear that it can carry as many meanings as it has comings and goings. Derisive remarks about this fact will do the tyro dragon-slayer no good.

The Churning of the Milky Ocean. Rajasthan miniature, Bikaner, late 17th century. Collection Edward Binney 3rd.

Illustration by Theodor de Bry to *Historia Americae* 1591–1634.

Engraving from Principio Fabrizi: *Delle allusioni, imprese et emblemi,* Rome, 1588.

Page from alchemical manuscript. Universiteitsbibliothek, Leiden, Ms. Voss. chy. F29, fol.94v.

Dragons and pearl. Mother-of-pearl inlay on a piece of furniture, Vietnam, 18th–19th century.

Zodiac of good and bad signs encircling the composite image of the universal cow mother and evil dragon. From Steffan Michelspacher: *Cabala, speculum artis et naturae*, 1654.

Engraving from Elias Ashmole: *Theatrum Chemicum Britannicum*, 1652.

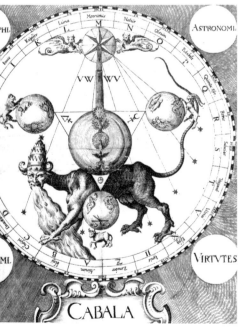

Lord of death

Humanity has spent a fair amount of its time pondering the fact that it is born to die, and asking whose fault it all is. Some lay the blame on the first man, or the first woman, or on a lying Devil; a few daring spirits go so far as to accuse God. Most agree there is a serpent involved somewhere, mainly on the grounds that it is one of the few creatures thought to live for ever, and to have the evil eye into the bargain. This makes it the proper guardian of those who have died, but who hope for the resurrection.

Statue of Aion from the Mithraeum at Ostia. Musei Vaticani, Rome.

Carving on wooden coffin from Zöbingen. Württembergisches Landesmuseum, Stuttgart.

Bearded snake. Greek relief. Staatliche Museen zu Berlin, D.D.R.

lord the black bull of death, who mounts corpses with sexual finality; above it can be seen an enigmatic face, crowned by five skulls, that is formed out of the hindquarters of a tiger skin and a writhing of serpents, whose coils make eyes. That this scene pictures the very entrails of Hell is confirmed by the Aztec codex, where a neatly tied-up corpse is sitting with its feet in the dragon's maw. It is about to make the great journey to the place where flesh and bone are to be disengaged from each other, so that the genius of life can slough off its mortality and the spirit free itself from matter. This spirit, with wedge-shaped noose and beaked mouth, is none other than Quetzalcoatl, the Feathered Serpent and god of wind. His mask of turquoise mosaic – which the emperor Moctezuma presented to Cortez on his arrival on the shores of Mexico, believing him to be the god himself – comprises two snakes, one blue, the other green, which epitomize his dwelling place in the sky and his time of sojourn on earth.

Yama, god of death. Gouache, Tibet, 1850–1900. Rijksmuseum voor Volkenkunde, Leiden.

Detail of the *Codex Laud,* Aztec manuscript. Bodleian Library, Oxford.

Turquoise mosaic skull. Aztec. British Museum, London.

Temptation of Adam and Eve, on font at Cotham. Line drawing from a rubbing. J. Romilly Allen: *Early Christian Symbolism in Great Britain and Ireland before the 13th Century,* 1887.

The Ophites held that the snake *was* God, in the sense that it came before all, and that the creator of this world was merely his misbegotten grandson, who should have known better. This snake can be seen coiling around the lion-headed Aion, whom the Mithraists took to be the emblem of time and of all that it brings forth and destroys.

Aion is a Greek word that denotes the sap of life, and hence a life-span; later it came to mean an epoch. The epoch of damnation in Tibet has as its principal

Some nasty pets

Those who have seen dragons at close quarters – and there are not a few alive today who claim to have done so – say that the spectacle filled them with a reverential loathing words can hardly express. 'Abominable' is a term they often use, just as the Babylonians gave to the fish-god who taught men the arts of civilization the name of Ea and the titles of 'the Repulsive' and 'the Abomination'.

It is hard to stomach the idea that civilization is the child of the abominable, just as the Abomination is the child of Tiamat – if that is she who is here shown with horns. It is even harder to live with the evident fact that civilization regularly offers sacrifice to the dragon in order to keep it quiet, though this does not at all stop it from growing larger. This is called 'setting a candle to the Devil', and the folly of this action is often celebrated with bravado and in a mock-show, to make it tolerable. Hence the once dangerous festivals of the dragon, and the villainous little brooch that the inhabitants of Tarascon wore in honour of their tutelary pet.

These games are now old-fashioned, and their stage properties – such as Snap the Dragon from Norwich, or the Dun Cow of Warwick – look as winsomely grotesque as the dinosaurs the Victorians set up around the Crystal Palace, to remind themselves of their evolutionary progress. The collage by Max Ernst shows the obvious place where the dragon was then at home, with the kind of hindsight that prophesies all kinds of liberation to come. Even that of the dragon, God help us.

facing page:

Neo-Babylonian dragon head. Mesopotamia, 7th–6th century BC Musée du Louvre, Paris.

The Dun Cow and the Property Master, Warwick Pageant.

Dinosaur models in grounds of Crystal Palace, Sydenham. 19th-century watercolour.

Snap the Dragon at Norwich, made in the early 19th century. Drawing from F.W. Fairholt: *Gog and Magog*, London 1859.

Tarasque plaque, Musée des arts et traditions populaires, Paris.

Demon attended by snakes and holding a trophy head. Vase-painting, Moche culture, c. 100 BC–800 AD. Drawing from Fernard Anton: *The Art of Ancient Peru*, London 1972.

Max Ernst engraving from *Une semaine de bonté*, 1963.

At the navel of the unborn

Before the appearance of Heaven and Earth, say the Egyptians, there was created a brood of serpents. Therefore,
Whatever you do, wherever you go,
Tread carefully, beware of the Oldest
of the Old!
Especially, the Egyptians would add, when you arrive in the Underworld and meet the Oldest and his wife, the serpent king and queen of that place. He has the crown of Lower Egypt on his head, and two pairs of legs to go with it; and, like his wife, a pair of royal vulture wings on which to fly to the Upperworld after he has finished his meal of carrion.

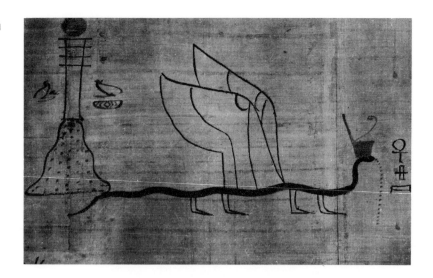

If your soul does not give him indigestion, he will serpentine you up to the sun where you will be remade of light.

The Hindus give to the Oldest the name of Vishnu, who wears upon his breast the brilliant wish-fulfilling jewel *Treasure-of-the-Ocean*. It is foretold that one day he will devour everything that is, and will become torpid after his tremendous feast. There will then be nothing left except himself, who is a snake, resting on what is called the Remainder, also a snake; and these two, who are each other, rest in turn in the Ocean of Milk, which also is none other than themselves.

Lost in his own coils, Vishnu is then said to be asleep. His dreams, when they come, garland the abyss with their festoons, and luxuriate into images of desire. At the navel of this universe the Oldest makes a wish and becomes the Youngest, and he is borne up as if on a lotus until he comes to the realm of action. There he awakes once more, entwined as ever by Kundalini, his female power, so that the cycles of birth and death may repeat themselves until that epoch ends.

'Unto us a child is born, unto us a son is given', says the Old Testament in heralding the New; a child who was

welcomed into the world by the massacre of the innocents. In like vein, an Aztec midwife – who knew as well as any the reeking sacrifices demanded by the gods – would say to the new-born: 'Oh precious stone, oh rich feather – thou wert made in the place where are the Great God and Goddess which are above the heavens. Thy mother and father, celestial man and woman, made and reared thee. Thou hast come into the world from afar, poor and weary. Our Lord Quetzalcoatl, who is the creator, has put into your dust a precious stone and a rich feather.'

facing page:

A section of Hell; from the funeral papyrus of Dirpu. Cairo Museum.

Vishnu with lotus. 7th-century relief in the Caverne de Dourgâ, Mâvalipouram, Madras Presidency.

Vishnu on the serpent of eternity. Khmer sculptured lintel in Angkor Wat Style. Musée Guimet, Paris.

this page:

Tomb painting from the Valley of the Kings, Thebes, New Kingdom period, 1738–1102 BC.

Vishnu, from folding book on Vaisnava legends. South India, 18th century. British Museum, London, Ms. Add. 155041, f.5.

Serpents encircling a mandala-yantra. Gouache on paper, Rajasthan, 18th century. Collection Ajit Moorkerjee.

Relief frieze of Xochicalco. Drawing by L. Castañeda from Kingsborough: Antiquities of Mexico, London, 1830–48.

Head of Tau cross. Walrus-ivory, English, mid-12th century. Victoria and Albert Museum, London.

Sources and further reading

Abbott, G.F., *Macedonian Folklore*, Cambridge, 1903.

Allen, R.H., *Star Names, their lore and meaning*, New York, 1963.

Bosch, F.D.K., *The Golden Germ*, The Hague, 1960.

Burnet, J., *Early Greek Philosophy*, London, 1892.

Campbell, J.F., *The Celtic Dragon Myth*, Edinburgh, 1911.

Campbell, J.G., *Superstitions of the Highlands and Islands*, Glasgow, 1900.

Cawte, E.C., *Ritual Animal Disguises*, London, 1978.

Coomaraswamy, A.K., *Hinduism and Buddhism*, New York, 1943.

Daniélou, A., *Hindu Polytheism*, London, 1964.

Dontenville, H., *La France Mythologique*, Paris, 1966.

Dumézil, G., *Le Festin d'Immortalité*, Paris, 1924; *Le Probléme des Centaures*, Paris, 1929; *Ouranos et Varuna*, Paris, 1934.

Dumont, L., *La Tarasque*, Paris 1951.

Eisler, R., *Orpheus – the Fisher*, London, 1921.

Frazer, J.G., *The Golden Bough*, London, 1911–15.

Frobenius, L., *The Voice of Africa*, London, 1913.

Gould, C. et al., *The Dragon*, London, 1977.

Granet, M., *La Civilisation Chinoise*, Paris, 1929; *La Pensée Chinoise*, Paris, 1934.

Graves, R., *The Greek Myths*, Harmondsworth, 1962.

Griaule, M., *Conversations with Ogotemmêli*, London, 1965.

Harrison, J., *Prolegomena to the Study of Greek Religion*, Cambridge, 1903.

Hartland, E.S., *The Legend of Perseus*, London, 1894–6.

Heidel, A., *The Babylonian Genesis*, Chicago and London, 1963.

Huxley, F., *The Way of the Sacred*, London, 1974.

Ingersoll, E., *Dragons and Dragon-lore*, New York, 1928.

Joralemon, P.D., *The Olmec Dragon*, Washington D.C., 1977.

Jung, C.G., *Psychology and Alchemy*, London and New York, 1953.

Kakouri, K.J.H., *Dionysiaka*, Athens, 1965.

Larson, G.J. (ed.), *Myth in Indo-European Antiquity*, Berkeley and London, 1974.

Lawson, J.C., *Modern Greek Folklore and Ancient Greek Religion*, New York, 1964.

Lindsay, J., *The Origins of Alchemy*, London 1970.

Neumann, E., *The Great Mother*, London 1955.

Portilla, M. Léon, *Aztec Thought and Culture*, Norman Okla., 1963.

Rees, A. and B., *Celtic Heritage*, London, 1961.

Reichel-Dolmatoff, G., *Amazonian Cosmos*, Chicago and London, 1971.

Roheim, G., *The Eternal Ones of the Dream*, New York, 1945.

Ross, A., *Pagan Celtic Britain*, London, 1967.

Rundell Clarke, R.T., *Myth and Symbol in Ancient Egypt*, London, 1959.

Santillana, G. de and Dechend H. von, *Hamlet's Mill*, London, 1969.

Séjourné, L., *Burning Water. Thought and Religion in Ancient Mexico*, London, 1956.

Smith, G. Elliot, *The Evolution of the Dragon*, Manchester and London, 1919.

Spinden, H.J., *Maya Art and Civilization*, Indian Hills, 1957.

Thompson, J.E., *Maya History and Religion*, Norman Okla., 1970.

Visser, M.W. de, *The Dragon in China and Japan*, Amsterdam, 1913.

Acknowledgments

Objects on the following pages reproduced by courtesy of Biblioteca Nazionale Centrale, Florence 44; Bibliothèque Nationale, Paris 45; Bodleian Library, Oxford 52; Trustees of the British Museum, London 37, 38; Cleveland Museum of Art, John L. Severance Fund 46; Kōzanji, Kyoto 56–7 upper; Museo Calouste Gulbenkian, Lisbon 60; Museo Nazionale, Taranto 50; National Gallery, London 47; Private collection 40–1, 52–3, 61; Smithsonian Institution, Freer Gallery of Art, Washington DC 58–9; Victoria and Albert Museum, London 42–3 lower, 48, 49, 62–3.

Photo illustrations on the following pages were supplied by Alinari 68 below r., 69 bottom, 85 below r.; Ferdinand Anton, Munich 67 above r.; Asia House Gallery, New York 83 bottom; Bord Failte Eireann 67 below r.; Paul Bryant-Camera Press 38–9; Chuzeville 79 above r.; Noel Cobb 64; Courtauld Institute of Art, London 79 bottom; Elsam Mann & Cooper Ltd 71 below r.; Chris Fawcett 56–7 below; Stephan Feuchtwang 76 top r., 77 below r.; Fine Arts Gallery of San Diego 88 top; Werner Forman Archive 34, 61, 78 above, 89 above r., 95 top; Gabinetto Fotografico Nazionale, Rome 51; Giraudon 78 centre; Sonia Halliday 36; Kodansha Limited, Tokyo 33; Kathie Konn 54–5; Eric J. Lantz 75 above; Mansell-Anderson 79; Mas 66 above; Leonard von Matt 50, 73 above r.; Musées Nationaux 72 above l., 87 above, 92 below l., 94 below l. and r.; National Monuments Record, London, courtesy B.T. Batsford Ltd 86 below; Andrei Pănoiu 40; Josephine Powell 35, 62, 67 below l., 72–3, 83 centre r., 87 below; Riksantikvaren, Oslo 75 below l.; Soprintendenza alle Antichità d'Etruria, Florence 86 centre; Spink & Son 52–3; Eileen Tweedy 40–1, 49, 65, 70 below; Jacques Verroust 42–3 above, 69 above r.; John Webb 63, 75 below r., 81 centre r.

Sources of illustrations on the following text pages: J. Romilly Allen, *Early Christian Symbolism in Great Britain and Ireland* 26; *Ancient Chinese Patterns* 29, 31; *Ancient Ships* plate II, no. 4, 24; Ferdinand Anton, *The Art of Ancient Peru* 28; Arnamagnean Collection, Copenhagen 20; Honoré de Balzac, *Les Contes Drolatiques* 18; British Library, London 30; Principio Fabrizi, *Delle allusioni, imprese et emblemi* 17, 23; Jan Filip, *Celtic Civilization and its Heritage*, New Horizons, Prague 6; Redrawn by Peter David Joralemon in *Origins of Religious Art and Iconography in Preclassic Mesoamerica*, UCLA Latin American Center Publications, from plates in V. Garth Norman: Izapa sculpture, part 1: album, *Papers of the New World Archaeological Foundation 30*, Brigham Young University, Provo, Utah 10 upper and 22 lower; *Rosarium Philosophorum* 14; Anne Ross, *Pagan Celtic Britain*, Routledge & Kegan Paul 25; Jacques Soustelle, *Arts of Ancient Mexico* after Sylvanus G. Morley, *The Ancient Maya*, Stanford, California 9 lower; H.J. Spinden, *Maya Art and Civilization* 8, 22 upper; Staatliche Graphische Sammlung, Munich 4